D1240081

THE EMOTIONAL JOURNEY OF SCOLIOSIS

THE EMOTIONAL JOURNEY OF SCOLIOSIS

FOR PARENTS DEALING WITH THEIR CHILDREN'S DIAGNOSIS OF ADOLESCENT IDIOPATHIC SCOLIOSIS

Reshmi Pal

First published on Kindle as an eBook "The Emotional Journey of Scoliosis", 2014

First print version- 2015

16-17Ing   16-17

Copyright © 2015 Reshmi Pal

Important Note

This book is not intended as a substitute for psychological or medical advice and treatment. Any person with a condition requiring medical or psychological attention should consult a qualified medical practitioner or suitable therapist.

ISBN 13: 9780992457211

ISBN 10: 0992457211

This book is dedicated to my husband and two lovely boys, who give me daily inspiration to stay above my circumstances.

'I am delighted to recommend Reshmi Pal's The Emotional Journey of Scoliosis. *As a registered psychologist and registered nurse who trained in the late 1960s and early 1970s, I remember with affection the Nightingale wards and the dedication of hospital-trained nurses. I believe the interweaving of Reshmi's personal journey and professional understanding and insights will help bridge gaps between clinical knowledge and an adolescent's lived experience of a physical and emotional journey. I am hopeful it will empower individuals, families and communities to more fully understand and utilise concepts such as constructive thinking, resilience and protective factors in life situations such as major surgery.'*

Lyn Cottier, RN, MA Psych (Family Therapy)

TABLE OF CONTENTS

Acknowledgements

I WOULD LIKE TO EXPRESS my sincere gratitude to all my surgeons and their teams for successfully performing my spinal surgeries, enabling me to achieve my lifetime goals and aspirations.

I was initially inspired to write this account of my personal journey by the theatre nurse who looked after me prior to my entry into the operating theatre for revision scoliosis surgery. This surgery was undertaken in 2006 in Sydney, Australia. While under preliminary sedation, I shared some of my experiences relating to my first spinal fusion, undertaken in 1974, which the theatre nurse found fascinating. She suggested I 'tell my story'.

I would also like to thank the following people who have either directly or indirectly contributed to the conception of this book:

My Aunt Roslyn, Canadian-born teacher and historian, who seeded the idea of this story while chronicling our ancestral family history and origins from India to

Fiji. She compiled each of the great-great-great-grand-children's stories, as well as suggesting we write our own.

Psychologist Dr Margaret Donnelly for reviewing the first draft in its embryonic stages and later drafts of this book; psychologist Lyn Cottier for helpful insights and suggestions on later drafts; and author Jo-Ann Berthelsen for her feedback on matters of writing. I would also like to sincerely thank my developmental editor, Glenda Downing, and copy editor, Dr Katy McDevitt, for all their assistance to get this book to publication.

I wish to thank Dr Peter McIlveen, Associate Professor, University of Queensland and editor of the *Australian Journal of Counselling Psychology*, who recommended that the essence of this book be submitted as a published paper, and encouraged me to publish my personal story in the near future.

This paper was published in a peer-reviewed journal, the Australian Journal of Counselling Psychology, in 2012. It was aimed at mental health professionals and intended to provide the profession with an understanding of the psychological and emotional implications of Adolescent Idiopathic Scoliosis (AIS, also referred to as scoliosis) on adolescents and their families. The paper can be accessed on my website under 'Publications' (www.palpsychology.com), and its details are also included in the reference section of this book.

I would like to acknowledge my special friend Sally, who underwent spinal treatment with me in 1974. Our unique experiences and her sense of humour created a special bond of friendship between us, and although we lost touch over the years we reunited in 2006.

Last but not least, I would like to thank my family: my husband for his tireless efforts in helping me bring my story from conception to completion and for his valuable feedback on the many drafts; and my children, who were endlessly patient as I laboured on this book for many hours at a time, and who helped me proofread the manuscript a number of times, especially from an adolescent's perspective.

INTRODUCTION

THIS BOOK CHRONICLES MY PERSONAL journey with scoliosis from adolescence to adulthood, and explores the challenges I faced after being diagnosed with scoliosis. It started as an autobiographical account for family and friends and then I felt a need to extend its use for parents whose children have been newly diagnosed. My hope is that this book will help inspire children, adolescents and parents whose lives scoliosis has affected.

I would like to say to the reader that I am a psychologist and not a writer. Writing this story from the perspectives of a child, an adolescent, an adult, a parent, a sufferer and a psychologist was a multifaceted task and a very challenging experience for me. It took countless hours of thinking and processing information before I finally put the various chapters together, not to mention that it raised memories of 1974, when I was first treated.

From the time of your diagnosis of scoliosis, you will find that you experience mixed emotions as you start to cope with what it all means. In the second part of this book, I help you understand why you feel the way that you feel and to recognise that many of your responses to scoliosis, from diagnosis to treatment, are entirely normal.

I would also like to pass on to the younger generation the hope, courage and determination they will need to face adversity. I say 'adversity' because, with adolescent scoliosis, a so-called normal spine at birth can suddenly start to curve when you reach early adolescence. This can be shocking and distressing, especially when you are advised that you need to have your scoliosis treated. But I want to reassure you that scoliosis is a condition that can be treated and, most importantly, that you can go on to live a normal life. Scoliosis is not an illness and therefore, it is important to have hope, and to remember too that scoliosis is only one aspect of your entire life.

In the 1970s, recuperation from surgery for AIS took a year. Today, treatment and recovery from surgery entail only a short hospital stay of approximately a week—very different to what I experienced in the mid-1970s. For parents whose children are required to undergo AIS surgery, this is an important consideration. Medical science has advanced significantly since the 1970s, and much more advanced pain control methods are also available today.

AIS is a type of scoliosis that emerges around early adolescence, and that most frequently occurs in adolescent girls. I was diagnosed with it in 1974 and was then required to undergo surgery in Australia. My case was exceptional because I needed further corrective surgeries in adulthood, which is far from the norm—my experience does not mean you will have the same. In fact, research indicates an excellent prognosis for people undergoing AIS surgery today.

Not everyone with scoliosis will require surgery, and the statistics bear this out: Scoliosis Australia indicates that scoliosis happens to one in 10 adolescent girls, of whom only two to three in 1000 need some treatment; of those who need treatment, approximately one in 1000 requires surgery. So, after diagnosis, a medical specialist will often recommend observation or bracing as the main treatment.

This book is in three parts with several easy-to-read chapters, designed to help you absorb the information it provides. Part I is my personal journey and Part II is a professional's perspective of the psychological implications of scoliosis. Part III contains perspectives from others around me.

Chapter 1 starts with my personal story, written from the voice of a 13-year-old undergoing AIS surgery in 1974. As the story unfolds, it culminates to an adult voice as I narrate undergoing corrective surgeries in adulthood. By sharing my story, I hope to demonstrate how far medical science has progressed since 1974, for those on the same journey. From this point, I go on to discuss the psychological and emotional aspects of scoliosis. You may decide to skip my personal story and go straight on to read the psychological aspects, if you wish.

Chapter 2 provides some medical information on scoliosis, giving a context to help you understand your emotional journey.

Chapter 3 looks at how adolescents may feel when they first find out they have scoliosis and require some form of treatment. It also acts as a guide to help you cope with your emotions.

Chapter 4 examines how those treated for scoliosis early on in life may feel on reaching adulthood, and discusses the possible impact of the diagnosis on you and your loved ones.

Chapter 5 is a guide for parents whose children have been diagnosed with scoliosis. It helps you understand your emotions and suggests some methods for coping with them; it offers advice for you and your child and guidance on how to help build their resilience. This section will also benefit parents whose children have types of scoliosis other than AIS, since parents share a universal emotional journey when their children are diagnosed.

Chapter 6 helps you recognise the symptoms that indicate counselling is necessary for both you and your family.

Chapter 7 is written from the perspectives of two people who are close to me: my husband, Yogi, who shares his experience of living with someone with scoliosis, and my good friend, Sally, who was a fellow inpatient at Margaret

Reid Hospital, Sydney, in 1974. Sally and I are still in contact today and share many recollections of the year we spent together as inpatients while we recuperated from surgery. Sally records some of our shared memories in her part of the book. Both these perspectives reveal one can go on to live a normal life.

References are included at the end of the book, including details of my *Australian Journal of Counselling Psychology* (2012) article.

While Chapter 1 of this book is based primarily on my personal experience with AIS over many years, the rest of the book contains information that incorporates the scientific training encountered in my profession as a psychologist. It is supported by many international research studies, which you can read about in my published paper.

You should note that this book does not discuss in depth the impact of more serious mental health issues or emotional disorders, and the interactions of such conditions and other existing ones with scoliosis. In all such instances, it is imperative that you consult with an appropriately qualified health or mental healthcare professional.

Finally, while I acknowledge that everyone's individual experience with scoliosis will be different, I hope that my personal story will inspire you and give you hope.

PART 1

~~

CHAPTER 1

MY PERSONAL JOURNEY

'Hope is the thing with feathers that
perches in the soul - and sings the tunes
without the words - and never stops at all.'

—EMILY DICKINSON 1830–1886

IT WAS 1974. THE DAY was warm and humid. The sun was still rising as I looked out the car window. Dew had started to evaporate from the palms and tropical fruit trees, and the exotic fragrance of frangipani was carried on the warm air. Mum and Dad were driving me to the airport, with my two sisters and my brother, for some sort of back surgery.

Before leaving home, I had glanced for one last time at our beautiful tropical gardens, which Mum and Dad had so lovingly tended—the anthurium lilies, the purple and orange orchids twining on balambalas, orange heliconias and dark purple bougainvillea climbing onto our porch area. I loved to arrange these flowers—it was one of my regular Saturday chores. In later years, I won many prizes in school contests and local festivals for my flower arrangements.

I was thinking how much I would miss the gardens and the beautiful lawns where I always played. The shrubs looked beautiful and colourful in the rising sun, and the palm trees waved majestically in the breeze. I loved watching them from my bedroom window, especially when they were bathed in the glow of the early morning sun and at sunset, when the palm leaves rustled in the wind.

I would miss summer holiday picnics on the lovely tropical beaches with my aunts, uncles and cousins. The family picnic was something my brother, sisters and I dearly looked forward to; we were very disappointed when the tropical rains came without warning and the picnic would have to be cancelled.

I remember waving goodbye to the housemaid, who was heartbroken for me. I had a lot of affection for her and liked to help her, especially when Mum was upset with her for not doing something the way she wanted. I would befriend the housemaid as she went about her chores, and she would cheer up once again.

Most of my aunts, uncles and cousins from Mum's side, who lived only across the road from us, had come to say farewell the day before I left. They knew I had to travel to Australia for surgery on my spine. I played with my cousins every weekend. There were no computers in those days and toys were scarce, so we made up a lot of games to play. I would miss them all. They did not think there was anything wrong with my back, and neither did I.

I had no problems with attending school and could do everything normally. Nothing looked different about me; I did not have any pain, so I did not understand what all the fuss was about. We did not know much about the surgery I required, except that it was quite urgent that I had it. The problem was identified when Mum took me to see a doctor for a routine medical check-up. It was discovered I had an abnormal curvature of the spine, called *scoliosis*.

Many tears were shed after Mum and Dad found out I needed surgery for my scoliosis; I had never seen Mum so upset. Mum and Dad were also not aware of anyone else who had this condition, let alone anyone who had needed to go overseas for treatment. It seemed as if I was a rare case (or at least, a privileged one), because my scoliosis was identified early and I was able to have treatment overseas. I can say, however, that even today not much has changed in assisting young adolescents and their families understand the need to be identified early and undergo treatment, if necessary, either because of a general lack of understanding of the importance of early identification by doctors, parents and the community at large, or lack of funding for school screening.

Since Mum was a primary school teacher and my Dad was also working, neither were able to accompany me to

Australia, and they also had my brother and two younger sisters to care for. Their inability to travel disheartened Mum and Dad even more.

At the time, I did not understand why exactly I needed surgery and, as a naive 13 year old, I simply followed the advice of the doctors, as did Mum and Dad. I did not fully understand that it would take a year to recuperate from the surgery and that I would be away from home for this entire time. Or perhaps it had not registered, even though Mum and Dad had advised me, given that I was forced to face everything so hurriedly.

I did not know then that, when I eventually returned home, I would need to do some things differently, or would not be able to do them at all. Of course, I was still going to be able to do many things I enjoyed, such as riding my bike and sitting cross-legged under the palm trees, with the breeze on my face, as I watched clouds form unique patterns and shapes—a favourite pastime as a little girl! But I would no longer be able to slide down the steep slope to the waterfall at the back of our yard after the spinal fusion I was required to have.

Sledding down to the waterfall in the midday sun was an activity I enjoyed with my brother, two sisters and our pet dog Scottie. Once at the bottom, I would wait to hear Mum's voice echo down the hill heralding me for lunch, pretending I could not hear her, responding only to find the look of exasperation I was all too familiar with. She knew how I lost track of time when I was at the waterfall, which always fascinated me. I liked to watch the cascade, surrounded by tropical wild bushes and flowers; the gentle stream meandering down with dry foliage and grass floating in it, amid tiny tadpoles and fish.

After Mum and Dad had finally made all the arrangements for my surgery in Australia, it was time for me to prepare to leave home. As they gathered everything for me and packed my luggage, they kept reassuring me they would visit me in Australia later that year when Mum was able to take leave from school. I could feel their sadness as they tried their best to stay cheerful for me.

On the way to the airport, I could feel Mum and Dad's distress once again. I looked at my brother and sisters; they were also miserable. No one spoke much. I do not think my brother and sisters understood much about *why* my surgery had to be done in Australia. Every so often, Mum gave me a worried glance; I noticed her voice quivered when she spoke. I was very close to Mum. We share the same birth date, which made birthdays extra special for us. Mum tried to give me hope as we drove on, and I felt encouraged.

When we finally arrived at the airport, it was time to say our goodbyes. Mum and Dad had told me that an air hostess would be in charge of me on the plane. Mum clutched me tightly with tear-filled eyes; Dad heartbroken, gave me last-minute advice, after which it was time for me to board the plane. I started to walk away from them, waving over my shoulder every so often. My brother and sisters quietly waved back.

As the plane finally took off, I remembered Mum's distraught face. I cannot remember being sad or dwelling on the thought of leaving them for such a long time— I think I was mostly oblivious to that fact. I was on the plane now and, as time passed, I was mindful of my surrounds and the hum of the plane's engines. I curiously observed everything outside the window and soon forgot why I was leaving home. I sometimes dwelt on Mum's sad face and wondered why she had been so teary and distressed after she found out about my surgery.

I was aware of the friendly air hostess checking on me many times during the journey, while I contentedly watched the fluffy clouds passing and felt the tilt of the plane as it climbed. After all, this was my first plane trip! Before long, the air hostess brought me a colouring book and pencils. I was very cross with her and thought: *doesn't she know I am 13 years old*? When she brought me crossword puzzles, I decided this was not for me either as I became travel-sick very easily.

I decided to continue watching the clouds. I loved their depth, their wispy, puffy formations and their constantly changing colours. After what seemed a long time, the plane prepared to land in Sydney. I was awe-struck by the red roofs of the houses beneath us as we swooped over them. I could not help thinking we would most certainly fall on the houses as we landed!

After collecting my luggage, the air hostess looked out for Uncle David, Mum's youngest brother who was a medical student in Sydney, and was to be my guardian for the year. Uncle David greeted me with his usual concerned smile and gladly took charge of me as the air hostess and I hugged and said our goodbyes. I always liked Uncle David when he came home to visit us from Australia, except when he called me 'Pigtails', because Mum tied my hair high in a ponytail!

As we exited the airport and drove away, I marvelled at the multi-lane roads. Everything looked different from home; the houses were different and the flowers were unusual but just as beautiful. I particularly liked the variety of blossoming trees; I remember thinking that I liked Australia.

MY FIRST SURGERY AT PRINCE OF WALES HOSPITAL- SYDNEY (1974)

A few days after my arrival, Uncle David admitted me to the Prince of Wales Hospital in Randwick, Sydney. My surgeon was the late Dr Keith Daymond. I met him only briefly before my surgery. At our first meeting, I noticed he walked with a stoop and carried a somewhat stern look on his face. He was speaking to the nurses about me; however, he did not look much at me.

I was angry that he did not address me; after all, I was the one having surgery and not the nurses! I knew I was only 13 years old, but I could understand what he was saying. Secretly, I decided I did not like him or his stern face! (In fact, Dr Daymond was a renowned surgeon of his time and I was in good hands, not that I knew at the time).

TRACTION BEFORE SURGERY

In the two weeks leading up to my spinal fusion surgery, I would be required to be in halo femoral traction. A halo is a metal ring placed around the head and attached to the skull bone with pins. During the traction, I was to be on a special bed called the 'rota-bed' (a very narrow bed, as narrow as an ironing board). Pins were to be placed in my knees with traction cords attached to these and the halo ring. Weights were to be attached at the ends of the cords. Every few days, the weights were to be increased to straighten out my spine or stretch it (I am not sure) before the placement of Harrington rods- a stainless steel surgical device to treat curvature and instability of the spine.

Upon waking from anaesthesia, I found myself in 'halo femoral traction' which I was in for two weeks. By the end of two weeks, I was pulled so straight I was un-able to see my meals and had difficulty feeding myself. I remember that sometimes Uncle David cut up my food to feed me, when he was able to get away early from his studies. All this time, I was required to lie very straight on my back, till the day of my spinal surgery.

On the 25th of October 1974, I underwent spinal fusion surgery with Harrington rods. After my surgery and upon waking up from anaesthesia, I recall being on the rota-bed once again. I remember vividly the excruciating pain I felt which is how I knew I had undergone surgery. I also noticed bloodstains on my fingers; it seemed theatre nurses had not cleaned me up properly! My spine was fused with two Harrington rods and other instrumentation. The fusion was performed from T8 to L3; that is, from the thoracic spine to my lumbar spine.

The fusion involved a bone graft. Bone for the graft was taken from the back of my waistline (a bone graft is when the surgeon takes strips of bone, to place between the bones of the spine to help with the fusion). I can remember having a lot of surgery pain after my spinal fusion, and receiving an injection of Pethidine every four hours for pain relief. I detested injections from a very young age, especially school immunisations, so I hated getting them.

On reflection, for a 13 year old I was dealing with a lot of pain, but at the time I just accepted it. I had no choice, as Mum and Dad were not there to support me. I think I was a strong child from a very young age, and in later years, Mum and Dad actually reminded me of this.

To take pressure off my surgery and the wound and to avoid bed sores, I was turned every few hours on the rota-bed. The nurses placed a mattress over me with an opening for the head area, strapped the mattress in three different places, counted to three and flipped me over either on my tummy or my back. I was turned every few hours in this 'sandwich' form for two or three weeks more. Every time I was turned, I experienced excruciating wound pain. It always made me break out in cold sweat; so much so, that I am wincing as I write this! It felt as though they were tearing my scar open. It took a long time for the pain to settle. The painkillers did not seem to work, and I would cringe when it was time for the 'turns'.

Each day, I had to eat at least one meal while I was lying on my tummy. I decided that whoever had invented bendy straws was very clever, as I had to sip drinks like this too. I remember that once, during a turn, I somehow got entangled midway through the turn; I was in agony until the nurses managed to untangle me. All this time, I was unable to get out of bed and did not like being pushed and pulled as the nurses changed my bedding. The nurses happily chatted away but I did not converse with them as I was in so much pain. They reminded me when my pain injections were due but I was not happy to wait as it always felt like an eternity.

In the midst of all this, I had what I call a 'guardian angel' watching over me each day. His name was Uncle Les. I didn't really know who he was, but he visited the children's ward at Prince of Wales Hospital, generously giving out gifts and speaking words of encouragement to the children in the ward. To this day, I have the modelling and painting sets he gave me and many other board games, as keepsakes from him. Uncle Les was often holding my hand when I woke up; he called me his 'little girl'. When I first woke up from anaesthesia after my surgery, it was Uncle Les who was holding my fingers tightly. He once wrote a letter to Mum and Dad about his empathy and compassion for 'his little girl' and his prayer that I would not miss them too much; I wish that Mum and Dad had kept the letter.

In my adult years, when I decided to enquire about Uncle Les, I was informed that he had passed on and a plaque in his memory had been placed at the Prince of Wales Hospital in Randwick, Sydney. I was sad at the news of his passing and remembered how Uncle Les had cared for me. I didn't know then that, in my university years during the 1980s, I would be fortunate enough to be great friends with Uncle Les's sister, Phyllis, who was residing right near my university in Randwick. Phyllis was not only my mentor but inspired me in many ways while I was at university. I remained great friends with her, until she passed away a few years after I was married which caused me a lot of grief.

At the time of my spinal surgery, I had no other family residing in Australia. I only have faint recollections of two of my aunts and uncles holidaying in Australia, visiting me at the Prince of Wales Hospital. I was excited to see them, but they also reminded me how much I missed Mum and Dad.

Mum wrote a letter to me every day just so that I could receive a letter from home daily, and of course, they were all excited whenever they received a note from me. My one and only regular visitor at the hospital was Uncle David, and I was always pleased to see him. Mum informed me later on, that a kind-hearted nurse had taken me under her wing all this time and had communicated with them regularly.

CONVALESCENCE AND REHABILITATION

About two weeks after my surgery, I was transferred from the Prince of Wales Hospital to Margaret Reid Orthopaedic Hospital (MROH) in St Ives, North Sydney, for my convalescence. I would now recuperate for a whole year in various plaster casts.

I remember that, when I arrived at MROH, the friendly matron greeted me and introduced me to the nurses. I noticed the nurses' white caps and the sisters' triangle tails on their caps, signifying seniority, as they busily attended to the patients. I also met many adolescent girls at different stages of scoliosis and other spinal treatments. Some of the girls were in 'bed plaster' casts, others in 'walking plaster' casts and still others in 'polythene jackets'. The girls and I became the greatest of friends as the year went on, and I started to feel happier as we shared our experiences.

My first cast was the 'bed plaster cast'—a hard cast, from my chest down to my pelvis. I was taken into a sterile room, where rehabilitation doctors started to wrap gauze around my chest and stomach and then down to my pelvis. After they had wrapped me up, they painted some sort of cold liquid over the gauze, patting and moulding strands of wet plaster around me. I did not like the feel or the smell of the cold liquid, and as the plaster cast started to dry and harden, I felt as though I could not breathe. I was not happy, and felt claustrophobic.

It took me a long time to get used to the hard cast, and I found it difficult to eat my meals because it fitted closely to my tummy. The bed plaster cast meant confinement to bed for the next three months. Over this time, we were required to use bedpans but, of course, with the cast all the way down to the pelvis, the girls and I found it hard to use bedpans and at night, the pans were very cold. We were lucky to get a warm pan. The male nurse made a point of bringing us warmer pans. We liked him for this and for sneaking us apples at night, when we were hungry after watching our late-night programs on TV.

While in the bed plaster cast, the girls and I survived staying in bed for three months by watching television the whole time. TV was in black and white in 1974. Some of the programs we watched were *The Walton's, John McDonald, Carson's Law, The Brady Bunch, Mike Walsh, Number 96, The Box* and *Young and Restless Years*—I was maturing fast!

The nurses kept records of the fluids we took, and so we were required to drink plenty through the day, which I did not like. To this day, the smell of lime, lemon and orange cordials remind me of MROH.

A local teacher provided tuition in Maths and English, although many of the girls often rebelled against the lessons. These girls were able to walk up to the table where the teacher had left his pipe, filling it with hair mousse or sometimes hiding his pipe just to annoy him. I could not participate as I was in the bed cast. The teacher thought I was a good student but I tried to hide my giggles! I also hated learning Maths.

All this time, I did not think too much about not being able to stand nor walk and liked the fun and friendship of the girls around me. Wards men turned us four-hourly from our backs onto our tummies and vice versa while in the bed plaster casts. In the early hours of the morning, there would be a turn and, being a light sleeper, I would anticipate that it was coming and found it hard to sleep. I also had to learn to sleep with my neck to the side while on my tummy for four hours at a time—I cannot do that now!

Hair-washing days were fun for all of us as nurses wheeled us one by one into the shower areas. We had to hang our heads over the trolleys while they washed our hair carefully, ensuring that water did not get on the cast or run down our backs. Afterwards, we were pushed outside on trolleys to help dry us, while we chatted and happily basked in the sunshine.

My best friend Sally and I remember when we grew up, that with our heavy body casts and no air conditioning, we found the summer heat difficult to cope with. It seemed that the only way nurses could cool us down was to wheel us outside to a paved area, where there was some shade. Sally remembered that if we were lucky a small breeze would help the nurses, who tried to cool us down with wet face-washers.

FRIENDS AND FAMILY

By this time, my surgery pain was slowly abating. I was getting used to Australia, the girls and my surrounds. All the girls, the nurses and I became the best of friends over this time; we all loved each other. I did not longingly watch planes traverse the sky, as I had when I first arrived. I was also thinking less and less about not being able to get out of bed for the three months, or about Mum and Dad not being there. The girls' parents made up for this by having a special affection for me. They made a point of coming to my bedside to ask after me, and I looked forward to their visits.

Just before I would have my next cast, my whole family was due to visit me in Australia. Mum was planning to take leave from school. I could not contain my excitement as I counted down the days and wrote regularly to Mum and Dad. I had to write the letters on a bed desk— a special tilted ledge the nurses placed over my chest, which we all used for meals and homework.

The months passed, and soon it was Christmas time, when my family finally came to visit me. They sailed on a boat called the *Arcadia* (so I missed out on a cruise!). But I didn't mind as I was in very high spirits. They too were so excited when they finally met with me; they could not stop fussing over me. I think Mum and Dad were surprised I was a picture of health, but my brother and sisters were disappointed, as I had to remain lying down and was not allowed to get out of bed.

I remember the nurses, the sisters and the girls' parents being excited and happy for me as they finally met my family. The parents became great friends with Mum and Dad as they all shared their stories. I remember the special Christmas lunch when everyone, including the parents and nurses, joined in. There was a lot of merriment and fun, and everyone made us feel special. No one seemed to care being in heavy body casts while there were so much fun and friendship around us!

As my bed plaster cast still restricted me to bed, I was disappointed that I was not able to walk with Mum and Dad in the hospital grounds, which had beautiful manicured lawns and colourful garden beds. Nonetheless, I was happy to have all my family there particularly my brother and sisters; they had missed me a lot.

After a month had passed, Dad and the rest of my family had to leave, but Mum stayed longer so that she could spend more time with me. The hospital's social worker organised for Mum to stay in the nurses' quarters for a time, just so Mum could be close to me, and afterwards she stayed with Uncle David in the eastern suburbs of Sydney. Of course, when it was time for Mum to return home too, I was very sad, but I cheered up with the help of the girls. Mum kept reminding me to stay strong and gave me her words of wisdom as she always did, to encourage me. I was heartbroken when Mum left, and missed my family hugely, but once again the girls came to my rescue, providing distractions and keeping me occupied and happy. Soon I was back to my normal self.

LEARNING TO WALK

At the end of three months in bed plaster, it was time to go into my next cast, which was the 'walking plaster' cast. I really looked forward to this cast, just so I could ride up and down my special bed. I had seen the girls in walking plaster casts using an electric tilt bed when I had first arrived at MROH, and I was excited now that my time had come. The girls autographed each other's casts—a common practice as the time came for them to go into the next cast. It was a fun experience accompanied by lots of laughter, and no one seemed to mind the prospect of yet another three months in the next cast!

The sound of the saw scared me at first when the old cast began to be drilled off, bits of it flying everywhere! Dead skin several millimetres thick had formed while the cast had been on. I was appalled at the smell of all that dead skin. Once I was cleaned up, I was wrapped up again with gauze, and then wet plaster applied layer upon layer, as before. Again, I had to patiently wait for my new cast to dry and harden. I hated the smell of the casts—both the old and new.

I cannot remember whether it was after the cast had dried or before it was put on that physiotherapists tried to stand me up, but sadly, I was unable to stand! My legs were like jelly and I would have fallen if it were not for the rails they had placed beside me. I could not believe I was unable to stand or walk. The muscles in my legs had weakened considerably over the four months of my treatment. So, despite my excitement over finally getting my special bed, I was very disheartened as I could not even walk! Physiotherapists had to teach me to stand and walk for a short distance each day. To get in and out of my bed, I had to stand on a special ledge attached to the front of the bed and strap myself to it before going up or down. Beds were going up and down the whole day for those of us in walking plaster casts trying to get in or out.

Once I could stand up and walk again, I was happy to be able to get around the ward and walk outside in the sunshine, where our trolleys would get pushed out on 'hair-wash' days. I felt enthralled at being able to visit the other girls confined in bed. But although I could walk, I was not permitted to sit for the next three months. I was only allowed to stand and lie down with this cast. I was not very happy about this!

I remember the walking plaster cast being thick and bulky; I looked like I was three times my size! We all found it difficult to figure out what to wear over the cast. I remember Mum had to have some of my nightdresses especially sewn with front openings, so that it fitted over my cast and I could sleep comfortably in it and take it off easily. Despite the difficulty, there was lots of fun and laughter; we also thought it was fun to knock on each other's casts as we passed each other.

After three months of wearing the walking plaster, it too was drilled off, after the girls had autographed the cast. I had to put up with the smell of dead skin once again! I then graduated into a hard polythene jacket, which fitted under my armpits down to my pelvis—this was the last stage of my spinal fusion treatment for scoliosis. I needed to wear this jacket for a further six months. This time, I was allowed to stand and walk but, again, I could sit for only a limited time.

By now, it was late 1974 and colour TV had just been introduced. Sally was the first to receive a colour set, and over time we all received one. With our awe and preoccupation with colour TV, the girls and I felt very contented and no longer minded our casts or polythene jackets, which was good for us!

After six months in the polythene jacket, I was allowed to return home. I was distraught at having to leave my friends and nurses at MROH, even more so than when I had first left home to come to Australia. I would miss them terribly—we had shared so much. Tears were shed once again; this time it was the nurses, the girls, their parents and I.

Uncle David was there as I said my farewells to everyone, after which he drove me to the airport. Looking back, I was grateful to Uncle David for taking guardianship of me and seeing me through my surgery. Today, he is a successful doctor and director of a busy medical practice in Sydney.

I remember that seats had to be vacated on the plane for me, so I could lie down for part of the four-hour flight home, as I was only able to sit for a limited time after my surgery. In total, it had taken 12 months to recuperate from my surgery for AIS in 1974— can you believe that?

RETURN HOME

As the plane neared landing I was reminded of all the girls and nurses, whom I started to miss terribly. As soon as I got out of the plane, I was aware of the familiar scents and humid air—aware of the nostalgic smell of home once again. I must add that, as I walked out of the plane, I also felt strangely different somehow—was it my strength of mind—I wondered? Or was it that I felt more mature, stronger and wiser—perhaps all of this.

When I was finally reunited with Mum and Dad, there are no words to describe how happy they were to have me back; tears freely flowed, Mum looking relieved and praying fervently. My brother and sisters were in high spirits to see me and would not leave my side. I had to reassure them that I was not about to leave again, and became quite impatient with their questions.

At first, I was not able to participate in many of my usual activities, as my 'up-time' was still limited. Our housemaid had to care for me and help me, as Mum was unable to take time off from teaching. As time went on, however, my up-time increased and, while there were still some things I could not do any more (like sledding down the hill), I was able to do most of the activities I did before. However, I really did not think much about what I could no longer do, and just did what I could do. After all, that was what mattered, I thought.

In terms of caring for my back, the doctors in Australia advised Mum and Dad to purchase a foam mattress for me to sleep on, so that I could lie as straight as possible. I was also given a 'helping hand'—a device that I could use to pick things up. I did not use the helping hand and thought it was a silly thing, but the device still exists some 40 years later! There was no further liaison with doctors in Australia.

RETURN TO SCHOOL

When it was time for me to return to school, Mum and Dad, following the advice of the surgeons, requested a comfortable chair, which they had to inspect before I started classes. Apart from that, I did not have any other knowledge on how to care for my spine, but I do remember that I was not allowed to lift anything heavy due to my fused spine. I felt uneasy when Dad dropped me off, as close as possible to my classroom so that I would not have to carry my heavy backpack; I pretended it did not bother me, but it did. I was also not allowed to play contact sports after my surgery, which I was not too happy about either.

At school, I was required to wear the polythene jacket for a short period after my return. I found this to be uncomfortable in the hot and humid weather. At this time, Mum had difficulty fitting uniforms over my brace and had to have them adjusted. Of course, wearing the polythene jacket I sat very straight in the chair and attracted the attention of the students. They stared at my straight back while in the polythene jacket and wanted to know why I was so straight. This did not bother me too much because I had an attitude of '*So what if they stare at me sometimes?*'; '*I am not going to let it bother me*'; '*They have the problem and not me!*' I think this was a good way for me to think about it all, as they were not able to make me feel bad about myself. But I have to say that I was relieved when my brace was eventually taken off.

In one instance, I recall the teacher having to explain to the class that I had undergone a special type of surgery for my spine and was not able to bend down to pick up things off the floor without kneeling down; the teacher encouraged my friends to help me out. I also did not have any other student to talk to about scoliosis, as nobody else at the school shared my experience. All this time, I tried to stay in contact with the girls in Australia; we wrote letters to each other regularly and sent post-cards, until our lives became busy with marriage and children and eventually we drifted apart.

Studying in Australia

In 1979, after I completed high school, I left home once again to study for my Higher School Certificate as a boarder at the Methodist Ladies College (MLC) in Burwood, Sydney. By now I was 17, and once again I found myself on a plane travelling alone to Australia; but of course memories of my previous trip for surgery had dimmed by now. This was the year that I learned a lot about 'being a lady'.

The mistresses at MLC were strict and made sure the rules of the school were followed or there would be con-sequences. What I particularly loathed was the shrill of the early morning bells, on chilly Sunday mornings, when we had to march up to the breakfast tables in time for church. The mistresses must have had eyes in the back of their heads—they picked up any mischief on our part, with disapproving looks. After breakfast we had to walk up to church on Burwood Road, Burwood in uniform, gloves and Panama hat. I remember boarders getting into trouble for not wearing gloves or hats in public. But while the mistresses at the boarding school were strict, I reluctantly admit that it led to the attainment of ladylike behaviours.

At MLC, I hardly thought about my scoliosis, and it gave me no problems. The only difficulties I experienced was not being able to participate in competitive house sports; I felt self-conscious about this, but otherwise I led a pretty normal life.

The year I spent at MLC was also the year that my Harrington rods came out. In the 1970s, it was customary for the rods to be removed five years after surgery. I have the discharge notes I requested later in life in 2006, from the Prince of Wales Hospital. The notes indicated I was in hospital for 10 days in 1979 for the removal of my rods. I am unable to recall the experience, perhaps because the brain efficiently suppresses painful memories. In the notes, I discovered, I had a 43-degree curve, which was corrected to 15 degrees after my treatment.

UNIVERSITY YEARS

On completing the HSC, I attended the University of New South Wales in Randwick, Sydney. During 1980, my first year at university, all was going well for me until I sustained a hairline fracture to my spine after jumping out of a window while cleaning it, and momentarily holding onto the windowsill without my feet reaching the ground. I was sharing a flat with university students at the time. As I realised afterwards, it can be hard to re-member that not everything is possible, or wise, when you have a fused spine. After I started to experience ex-cruciating pain, and on consulting with doctors at the Prince of Wales Hospital, I was advised I needed to wear my polythene jacket once again, for approximately three months.

I was very disappointed as I was attending university and felt self-conscious about having to wear the hard jacket. Some of the students in my tutorials stared at me, as I sat so straight. I also did not like anyone coming close to me in case they discovered I was wearing a hard brace. I have to say wearing the brace knocked my confidence at university and I was even more self-conscious when around the opposite sex.

Apart from this setback, I did not have any further problems in the later years of university and in 1984 I completed my postgraduate studies in Psychology and Education at UNSW. The following year I commenced my career as a psychologist.

PARTNERING IN LIFE
When I first met Yogi, who was later to become my hus-band, I was hesitant to tell him about my scoliosis. After plucking up the courage I told him. I found him to be reassuring and caring. Our relationship continued to blossom. It was evident that he loved me for who I was—scoliosis was not going to affect our relationship. He

accepted it as a part of me, and I was happy. We married in 1988 and moved to live in Melbourne. I was working long hours and my role required me to travel a fair bit. I thought very little about my scoliosis all this time and lived a pretty normal life.

After two years in Melbourne, Yogi and I moved to Sydney. As a young psychologist, I could not help feeling that my extraordinary journey with scoliosis had prepared me well for this profession. The importance of life experience cannot be underestimated in becoming an authentic psychologist. By now, I felt I had an acceptance for life and toughness of mind which enabled me to deal with anything.

STARTING A FAMILY

In 1991, I had my first child—a normal delivery—and my second in 1993. During both of my pregnancies, I experienced slowly increasing back pain. Of course, I could have greatly benefited from taking more regular rest, particularly since I had a fused spine; but at times I found it hard to slow down. Not easy to do when you are a perfectionist, I must add.

For my second baby, I elected to have a caesarean section due to the back pain and stress on my spine I experienced with my first baby. I found this to be a good decision. Having elected to have a C-section for the second pregnancy, there was no pressure on my spine during delivery and, consequently, less back pain. Considering my spinal condition and the back pain I experienced with the normal delivery, I should have consulted my spinal surgeon on the best method of delivery for both pregnancies in the first instance—a lesson learned! Overall, I was glad to have an extremely competent obstetrician and was confident in his care.

I was elated to have two lovely boys, especially when I learned years later that some of my friends at MROH had been advised not to have children at all. This is certainly not the advice given now, so have no doubt that you *can* go on to have children even with scoliosis.

From 1993 to 2000, I juggled a young family and my career and, by this time, the demands on my spine were most certainly increasing. I found that lowering my perfectionist standards, which I inherited from Mum, helped me to cope at home. Although my pain threshold was high and I could do everything as normal, I found I had to prioritise my days so I did not place undue stress on my spine. My husband also shared the responsibilities of parenting and managing a home, which helped enormously.

All this time, I loved being a mum and managed to foster a fun and happy atmosphere for the children. The two boys were the joy and delight of my life. I found meaning in being a mother; it helped to reduce focus on 'me and my scoliosis', giving significance to my life in many other ways. Having a meaningful job that I was passionate about was helpful and, again, reduced the focus on myself. It does not mean I did not care about my scoliosis, but my attention on other things helped to prevent me obsessing over my condition.

SECOND ROUND OF INTERVENTIONS

By the year 2001, although I was coping well, I started to experience progressively increasing pain in my lumbar spine. I tried to contact my surgeon but was informed he was deceased. I was saddened by the news and yet grateful for everything he had done for me. Yogi and I decided to look for another surgeon to care for me who specialised in scoliosis. We managed to find a new surgeon, who monitored me for a few years, but who then retired. I then had to find yet another surgeon and this time, found one who not only had specialist knowledge of scoliosis but has undertaken extensive research on scoliosis over many years.

This surgeon, Professor T.K.F. Taylor, informed me that AIS travels predominantly down the female gene and mostly affects adolescent girls. He also indicated that it had some correlation with high intellect! I knew the former was probably right and informed him I could not confirm the latter. Professor Taylor monitored me for several years and advised me of the importance of engaging in a program of isometric exercises to improve my core muscles as well as improve postural control. He indicated that I should swim 'no matter what: rain, hail or shine' to improve muscle tone, but with the business of children, home and work I found this difficult.

From 2004 to 2006, my pain levels grew more pronounced, especially when I needed to sit or stand for prolonged periods. One day in May 2006, after a family lunch, I was lying in bed on my side and suddenly found I could not get out of bed. Over the ensuing weeks, it became increasingly difficult to walk and my up-time kept reducing. I made it to my surgeon in a bundle of nerves and awaited his perusal of the X-rays with bated breath. After what seemed like an eternity, he advised quietly I would need scoliosis surgery to correct a translation of the L3 disc on L4. With my predisposition to disc degeneration, Professor Taylor recommended the current fusion be extended to the sacrum which would, of course, mean a very rigid spine and limitations on mobility.

My heart skipped a beat at this news; I felt a chill wind at the idea of a second spinal fusion, after all that I had been through in 1974! Since Professor Taylor was no longer performing surgeries but working purely in a consultancy role, he had to refer me to another orthopaedic and spinal surgeon for consideration of further surgery. I was informed that the surgeon I was being referred to would be able to undertake this very rare type of surgery and on a spine that had already been fused.

This was the commencement of the second round of surgeries for my spine. I am not sure how to describe my emotional state—a combination of shock, disillusionment, disappointment and angry feelings. I pondered if I could have controlled this sequence of events. If any of the earlier surgeons had indicated I was heading for further surgery, would I have been more diligent about my fitness and activity levels? Would I have more carefully restricted the bending and twisting motions involved in caring for my children? I felt strong, mixed emotions and, of course, a sense of guilt that I had not taken sufficient care of my spine. I could not help thinking there was something I could have done differently but, in reality, the problem I had was a structural one, over which I had little control.

At this time, I also started to experience vivid flashbacks of my first surgery in 1974. I had to keep reminding myself not to lose hope but to keep perspective. I felt more hopeful and reassured when my surgeon explained the details of the surgery, including the small amount of time I would spend in hospital this time compared to my 1974 surgery, and the fact that I could recuperate at home with family and friends.

By now, all my family lived in Australia. I reflected on what I had been through decades earlier and considered it in the light of advances in medical science, which helped me to accept the surgery. The revision scoliosis surgery would, however, entail having rods in my spine yet again. Would I ever have thought this would happen again? Of course not.

As each day passed, I came to realise the importance of staying positive and hopeful. I think that, by nature, I have an optimistic personality style but at times I felt disheartened. I consoled myself by thinking that things could have been worse, and I reminded myself to take one step at a time. By this stage in my life, I had progressed to working as a psychologist in private practice. I was pleased to have achieved a lot, both personally and professionally. I felt privileged to have two lovely boys who give me daily inspiration to stay above my circumstances. I also relied heavily on my Christian faith which mum had instilled in me from early on in life.

Revision Surgery

My revision spinal fusion took place in August 2006. Before I entered theatre, and while under preliminary sedation, recollections of 32 years earlier flitted across my mind. I started to shiver uncontrollably. On the way to the operating theatre, I shared some of my experiences of the 1974 surgery with the theatre nurse. She thought what I had shared with her was fascinating and suggested 'I tell my story'. She inspired me to write this book.

As the anaesthetist prepared to insert an intravenous cannula to start anaesthesia, I was unable to explain what I was experiencing, but he noticed I was shaking like a leaf. He asked whether I was cold, and as I only managed a feeble response, he covered me with special thermal blankets. My surgeon entered the room, asking what was going on. I smiled drowsily before falling asleep; I was unable to explain I was reliving vivid memories of my 1974 surgery.

My surgery was successful; I had a posterior spinal fusion. Titanium rod implants and other surgical instrumentation were utilised to correct the curve, with bone grafts taken from my right hip. The operation took approximately 5–6 hours. I had to have a blood transfusion. On waking up in intensive care, I was quite overwhelmed, as I drowsily observed myself hooked up to all the monitors and other gadgets. The one consolation was that I was not on a rota-bed!

The nurses showed me how to self-medicate for pain relief. I had an intravenous drip and could control the amount of medication by myself to manage my pain levels. I think I coped better with the pain than I had in 1974, but I have to say that I did not cope well with the nausea, which stayed around for a while. I was given anti-nausea medication to help relieve this. At times, I think the nausea was even worse than the surgery pain.

I was made to stand in intensive care after only the second day of my surgery— but still with a lot of nausea. What a difference compared to not being able to stand up for three months post-surgery 32 years ago! I was in intensive care for two days and, by the third day I was in my own room, sitting up with the help of painkillers. In total, I was in hospital for only 10 days.

By day three, physiotherapists were taking me for a walk at least twice a day. I was only able to walk a short distance and take only very small steps initially, which gradually improved. With my daily walks, and given the heavy painkillers, I was easily fatigued and slept most of the day. But each day I felt exhilarated with my rapid progress.

I was very grateful to my surgeon when I saw my X-rays and what had been accomplished. I realised that he was an amazing surgeon—a 'carpenter', in his words. Spinal fusion surgery is a very complex surgery. There is always the risk of nerve damage, paralysis and even a non-union, but there are many extremely skilled surgeons who can competently perform such surgeries.

My sitting and standing tolerances were limited after my surgery. I was only able to be up for an hour at a time, which gradually increased as my spine became stronger. After my surgery, I was not permitted to lift anything heavy, nor to bend or twist my spine in any way. I had to wear a brace to support my spine and allow the fusion to solidify but after three months, it was no longer necessary to wear the brace.

Post-surgery, I put myself through intensive rehabilitation. I started with gentle hydrotherapy exercises, which then transitioned to swimming. Over the following two years—from 2006 to 2008—I managed to swim one kilometre three times a week. I found that exercising regularly not only helped strengthen my spine but also lifted my moods—something psychologists generally encourage.

My immediate family needed to make a lot of adjustments over this time. For instance, with my limited up-time, I was unable to prepare family dinners on the days I worked. I was also unable to do any housework, so we hired a housekeeper. My husband had to undertake the responsibilities of both parents. Our social life needed to be restructured. I was also unable to do many of the things I had previously taken for granted due to my very stiff spine, such as kick a ball or swim in the surf with the boys, who at the time were 13 and 15 years old. I think I felt more aggrieved by this than the boys did.

I have to say that the boys were remarkably strong for me all this time. Having to do a lot of things independently of me built their self-efficacy. Witnessing their mother coping with spinal problems and having to deal with this from when they were young taught them acceptance. Today, both boys are resilient young men with an air of determination about them.

In April 2008, my surgeon performed the second phase of the surgery to remove part of the instrumentation placed in 2006, namely the prominent rod connectors. This was to be my fourth surgery. My surgeon and his team performed the surgery successfully. The rest of the rods in my lumbar spine will remain, which means, of course, that I must be careful not to stress my spine.

Sometimes rods can move or break and have to be replaced through further surgery.

At the time of my further surgeries, I tried to contact my friends from MROH, with whom I had lost touch over the years. I managed to locate two of them through internet searches, which was tremendously exciting—Sally, my best friend from MROH, was in Queensland, and another friend was in Canberra. It was great to catch up with them after so many years. Tears welled as we reminisced about MROH. Our memories were so vivid it felt as if we were discussing events of only a week ago. Their parents also spoke on the phone with me of their own memories.

Neither of my friends proceeded to have children, following advice from doctors that a fused spine would entail being confined to bed from the sixth month of any pregnancy. One of them was advised not to have children at all, which is not the advice given today. I felt blessed to have two lovely children.

All was not over for me, though. Approximately four months after part of my instrumentation was removed, I started to experience a stinging sensation around my lumbar spine area, which interfered with my swimming. At first, it was not clear whether this was residual pain from surgery, but the condition gradually worsened and I needed bone and CT scans to further investigate the problem. The results revealed a non-union in the L1 and L2 junction, which is the lumbar spine. I was previously instrumented in this area, but it now showed a crack through the fusion mass and an ongoing non-union. I was advised I would require a third fusion to fix this problem.

I felt trapped in a vicious circle, and my heart sank. Once again, I had a lot of mixed emotions. It had taken me two years to get to where I was. Although my progress after the last surgery had been at a snail's pace, I had come a long way and once again, I had resumed my career. Hence, I was dismayed with the forthcoming interruptions. I knew that over time I would have to work on acceptance, staying hopeful and remaining positive.

By 'staying positive', I mean thinking in constructive ways even when I did not feel like doing so. I have to say that, at times, the whole experience seemed so unfair; it was easy to feel hopeless and helpless. I remembered Mum's wise words: "even in our darkest moments, there are gems to be found".

I tried to keep myself gainfully occupied to keep my mind off myself. I accomplished this by starting to write this book, as well as researching for my paper, on the psychological implications of scoliosis, which was subsequently published in a peer-reviewed journal of psychology in 2012.

FURTHER SURGERY
In early 2010, I agreed to undergo further surgery, as the pain had started to interfere with my day-to-day

activities. By this time, I was swimming regularly and had increased my working hours. I decided to stay determined although my coping skills were getting somewhat strained. I convinced myself I had to get through this. It would be unlike my 1974 experience and after all, what other choice did I have?

In April 2010, I underwent the third spinal fusion. This time, the surgeon had to perform an anterior fusion, making an incision at the side of the chest wall and working on the front of the spine through the chest wall and abdomen. The fusion was undertaken at L1-L2 with instrumentation as before. My lower ribs were removed for bone grafting.

As I mentioned previously, a spinal fusion is major surgery, and it is paramount to find a skilled surgeon in whom you have confidence.

Once again, I wore a brace for three months. This was to help prevent the fusion failing and to allow the fusion to solidify. After my brace came off, I was unable to stand for more than an hour initially, and then gradually increased to up to three hours at once, over a period of a year. I had worked so hard to rehabilitate myself after my 2006 and 2008 surgeries that I felt disheartened to have to start all over again. However, I was comforted by the knowledge that now my children were in their teens, they were able to care for themselves and drive to school.

After my discharge from hospital, the strong pain-killers made me very drowsy and I slept for most of the day. The pain from my anterior surgery took a long time to subside. The anaesthetist advised me that I would have residual pain from this for quite some time; I think he was correct in saying this.

HAVING HOPE

After the surgery, I decided to put my heart and soul into my rehabilitation in an attempt to resume a normal life once again. While I had built an inner strength, I also recognized the importance of staying hopeful and determined. Focusing beyond the surgery was essential—I made the decision to stay above my circumstances. After all, things could have been worse. Mum kept reminding me to have hope, and I have to emphasise how important it is to remember this when things feel hopeless.

My husband and the rest of my immediate family tried to stay positive for me, and I clung to their hopes for me. Their positivity helped me to stay positive. But they also needed a lot of support over this period—multiple spinal surgeries can take an emotional toll on the whole family, who require both emotional and physical support. I know that my husband often struggled to look after me while managing the household and the boys and carrying his own work commitments. Things were not particularly easy for him. Our good friends provided ongoing emotional support and offered to prepare our meals, do our ironing or help with anything else we required. As we found, good friends and family support was essential.

After three months in the brace, I was determined to return to work, but needed to make many adjustments to my lifestyle. My husband took on the roles of both parents once again, demonstrating the importance of having a caring and considerate partner.

COPING PHYSICALLY

As I managed to build my fitness levels, I was gradually able to get back to normal levels of functioning. Personally, I found general back strengthening and endurance exercises helpful, including core muscle strengthening exercises. I regularly swam freestyle and breaststroke, which helped further strengthen my back. I have continued with these activities since my 2006 surgery.

It is to be expected however, that with multiple spinal surgeries there can often be residual pain which needs to be managed. I found a heated hydrotherapy pool not only helped soothe my spine but was the best way to undertake most of my exercises. Engagement in these activities proved rewarding, also providing gainful occupation of time. I also made many adjustments to my lifestyle in order not to stress my spine unnecessarily.

Despite my uphill battle with multiple spinal surgeries, my husband and children, and of course my great friends, all inspired me to stay above my circumstances. My two boys provided me with daily inspiration to stay grounded and not lose focus on my recovery. Today, I am proud that both boys are studying at Sydney University, one nearing completion of his studies. I feel privileged to have travelled part of my journey with scoliosis with the boys. I have witnessed many qualities in the boys, such as resilience and strength of character that I mentioned earlier.

Recovery from spinal fusion, which is a complex surgery, can be a long and demanding process. Personally, I can say I have had many lessons in patience, perseverance and hope. After five back surgeries, including three spinal fusions, I have a long way to go and need to stay focused on caring for my spine. I have decided there is nothing worse than dwelling on what you *cannot* do; there is so much you *can* do even with scoliosis.

Remember that if you require surgery for your scoliosis, with advances in medical science today, and the highly advanced skills and knowledge of competent surgeons, you can proceed with confidence. Also take note of what my surgeon told me: that AIS can travel down the female genes (although in my case the link appears to have been broken, at least on my side of the family).

COPING EMOTIONALLY

Reflecting on my overall experience with scoliosis, I decided that my scoliosis does not define me. I *have* scoliosis, but it is not going to manage me—I am going to manage it. Scoliosis is something that happens to you—it is not you. Beauty comes from within a person and who they are, not from how they look. Having a bad back taught me to have the right attitude to life. I would much rather this than have a normal back and a bad attitude to life, as my best friend Sally had rightly said.

Overall, my experience has taught me to stay above my circumstances no matter what; to face life with courage and determination, and never to lose hope that things will get better. Whether you face a medical condition or some other adversity, it can often be difficult to accept the situation, while also dwelling on what could have been or even questioning 'Why me?' At first, it is not easy to stay positive and hopeful but it is essential to work on acceptance and staying grounded.

It is imperative to acknowledge that change is very much a part of life and that everyone at some stage in life needs to deal with it. His Holiness the Dalai Lama says that suffering is part of living and that it can bring to light our best parts as a person and help make us stronger. When we have to cope with adversity, it can sometimes be hard to think of inner strengths that can help us survive. I found that, as I endured physical pain, my strength of mind in turn became stronger.

Reminding ourselves of our inherent strengths, such as hope, courage and determination, and practising gratitude for what we do have, not only enhance our coping skills but can build our resilience. Remember that we all cope differently, and different people will do different things to help them cope. For Mum, a reliance on her Christian faith and inner strength helped her cope. She instilled the same in me, which in turn helped me.

Finding meaning and purpose in life is important in order to stay grounded—a meaningful career, a nurturing family, valued friendships, and a focus and reliance on deeper values in life, such as your spiritual values or a reliance on God can help you stay above your circumstances. Remember, there is so much more to life than your scoliosis!

I will say my journey with scoliosis changed my personality in many positive ways: the trials I went through gave me an opportunity to grow in wisdom, maturity and character so I can offer strength, encouragement and hope to others, and reach out with compassion to people in pain. Most of all, it helped develop my resilience and make me who I am today. I learned to be courageous and determined, and to face up to adverse circumstances with hope. You need to step up to scoliosis with inner strength and learn to be a survivor!

SOME FINAL THOUGHTS

Everyone's journey with scoliosis will be different. Up to now, you have been reading my personal journey with scoliosis. It is essential for you to keep in mind that my case is unusual for those who have surgery for AIS. Most individuals diagnosed with AIS will not face surgical intervention, let alone undergo multiple surgeries as I did. Research indicates an excellent prognosis for AIS surgery, as I mentioned at the beginning of this book, and further surgeries are rarely needed.

However, if you are facing surgery for AIS, remember to take into account the fact that medical science has come a long way in recent decades. Today, surgical intervention for AIS does not entail plaster casts or confinement in bed—your treatment for scoliosis will be very different to what I experienced all those years ago. Your stay in hospital will also be very short. If you do need to have surgery, consider this and take the steps towards surgery calmly and confidently. Do not lose hope! Remember, hope is the single most important thing—so focus on this.

In the following chapters, I will provide some medical information on scoliosis before discussing the psychological and emotional implications of scoliosis.

PART II

~

CHAPTER 2

MEDICAL INFORMATION ABOUT SCOLIOSIS

WHAT IS SCOLIOSIS?

IN THIS CHAPTER, I WILL provide a brief overview of sco-liosis, to enable you to understand what it is and to provide a context for later discussion of the psychological and emotional implications of scoliosis. Here, I will mostly discuss AIS, the form of scoliosis I have personally experienced. There is a wealth of information on the different types and causes of scoliosis you can read about on reputable sites on the internet.

Scoliosis is an abnormal curvature of the spine, which can affect children, adolescents and adults. Scoliosis is cat-egorised by different age groups into infantile idiopathic scoliosis (0–2 years), juvenile idiopathic scoliosis (3–10 years) and AIS (11–17 years). Scoliosis can also impact in adulthood, both in people whose scoliosis was not identi-fied in adolescence, or whose curves progressed over time due, for instance, to degenerative changes such as disc degenerative disease or osteoporosis (a condition that affects the bones causing them to be weak and fragile).

Scoliosis is not a disease or an illness, but simply a condition, where the spine starts to both, bend and twist in an abnormal way. Research indicates that there are several different causes of scoliosis, but the exact cause is still not known. Many studies indicate that scoliosis can run in families, so the children and siblings of someone who has been treated for adolescent scoliosis, particularly with surgery, should be screened. Ongoing research on scoliosis continues to expand the overall understanding of this condition.

ADOLESCENT IDIOPATHIC SCOLIOSIS (AIS)

'Idiopathic' refers to a condition for which the cause is unknown. AIS is a type of scoliosis that generally emerges in early adolescence as the name suggests, and mostly affects adolescent girls. Research indicates that scoliosis in adolescence can often increase at around the time you reach puberty because of the growth spurt that takes place at that time. The most obvious symptoms can be uneven hip and shoulder heights.

HOW SCOLIOSIS IS DETECTED

It is not always easy to detect scoliosis, as you may not experience pain or other symptoms. Sometimes, the only way that it is detectable is when your parents or your doctor notices that you have uneven hips and shoulder heights or a hump in your back. If a doctor diagnoses the condition, they will refer you to a spinal specialist who will advise on the best method of treatment for you.

Adolescent scoliosis can also be detected by what is called a 'school screen', under a special program called the National Self-Detection Program for Scoliosis. This program was introduced by the Spine Society of Australia with the assistance from the Australian College of General Practitioners to help the earlier detection of scoliosis in schools in Australia. Australian schools are encouraged to participate in the program to help with earlier detection of scoliosis. Complete Information on scoliosis and the early detection is available on the Scoliosis Australia website *(www.scoliosis-australia.org)*. Today, community awareness of scoliosis is still growing, and needs to continue to increase, so that those identified with scoliosis are able to understand the need for earlier detection and treatment.

HOW SCOLIOSIS CAN AFFECT YOU

If scoliosis is left untreated and the curvature progresses, it can lead to medical complications, and it can even cause a change in the appearance of the spine over time. Adolescents can particularly be self-conscious about how AIS affects their appearance, as their spine may obviously change. Many studies have indicated that when scoliosis leads to an obvious curvature of the spine, people commonly experience concerns about their body and how it looks, and may even compare themselves with their peers.

Physical appearance in general, particularly in adolescence, can become an important factor, determining how a person feels about their body and hence, how they feel about themselves overall. Many studies indicate that adolescence is a stage of life when many other physical and psychological changes occur in the body. In combination, this can make someone diagnosed with scoliosis that requires treatment feel overwhelmed. It is important to obtain counselling assistance if your diagnosis is making you feel this way, and we will come back to this later in the book.

TREATMENT FOR ADOLESCENT SCOLIOSIS

The treatment for scoliosis depends on the type of scoliosis, degree of curvature, age of the person at diagnosis and the rate at which the curvature progresses. Someone who has only mild scoliosis may find that it does not affect them in any way, but someone with severe scoliosis can find that it will have an impact on how much they can do over time. Treatment for scoliosis will stop the curve from progressing further and reduce the likelihood of pain connected with the condition. It can also help prevent associated medical problems later in life. Treatment for your scoliosis will ensure that you have a straight spine and may therefore improve how you look and feel. In adolescence, treatment for scoliosis can improve your self–esteem and self-confidence at a stage in life when issues of physical appearance and fitting in with peers can affect many people.

TREATMENT METHODS FOR ADOLESCENT SCOLIOSIS

Since everyone's case of scoliosis is different, the treatment required will also be different. Generally, spinal specialists treat scoliosis via three different methods. The first is observation, where a doctor monitors the curve; the second is wearing a brace for a period of time; and the third is surgery. Remember that with appropriate and early treatment for your scoliosis, you can go on to live a full and normal life.

BRACING FOR AIS

Research indicates that most people with AIS are treated by bracing. This means you need to wear a brace to school for a period of time that is agreed between you and your doctor, under the care of your doctor. Sometimes, even after bracing, surgery may be required.

SURGERY FOR AIS

Where surgery is required, a spinal fusion is performed to halt the progression of the curve. This is done through the insertion of metal implants and bone grafts. In some cases, a brace may be needed for a short period after surgery to give the fusion the best chance to heal and solidify as well as support the spine. For the purposes of surgery, a hospital stay of approximately one week is required.

Alternative treatment
Since surgery is the most intrusive treatment method, parents sometimes seek information on alternative treatment for scoliosis. In this case, parents sometimes consider postural correction methods and movement awareness training, such as the Schroth Method, the Feldenkrais Method, and Alexander Technique to name a few. However, it is essential to discuss all options with a spinal specialist, particularly concerning the prognosis of any alternative treatment methods for your individual case.

In my own case, I recall that during my time recuperating at MROH, the physiotherapists commented that my spinal curvature was only minor, and could have been corrected by physiotherapy, while my surgeon advised that structural scoliosis needs correction via bracing or surgery.

Psychological implications
In the following chapters, I will provide you with a guide to understanding the psychological and emotional

implications of scoliosis, especially when treatment is required. The information contained in this section is based on my personal experience and supported by international research studies in medical and psychology journals. Most of these sources were also used for the paper I published in *the Australian Journal of Counselling Psychology*.

The information provided here is to help guide the person diagnosed, parents and loved ones from diagnosis to treatment. The primary purpose is to inform you and build your awareness of the psychological impact of scoliosis throughout your life. Although I will mostly refer to AIS, the information in this section may also help parents whose children have other types of scoliosis, as the emotional response to the diagnosis of scoliosis is in some ways universal.

Please remember that this information is intended as a guide, and is by no means comprehensive. As such, it cannot be used as a substitute for formal diagnosis or treatment. You should seek professional advice from an appropriate mental health professional for your individual situation, by which I mean a professional such as a school counsellor, social worker, psychologist or another suitably trained mental health professional.

As you read the following chapters, keep in mind that when you first gather information on a medical condition and start to gain awareness and an understanding, you may find the information overwhelming. However, it is helpful to remind yourself that information can also reduce apprehension and empower you, so try to focus on those benefits.

~

~ૢ

CHAPTER 3

SCOLIOSIS AND EMOTIONS IN ADOLESCENCE

'It's not whether you get knocked
down; it's whether you get back up'

—VINCENT LOMBARDI

COMMON RESPONSES TO DIAGNOSIS OF SCOLIOSIS

EVERYONE WHO IS DIAGNOSED WITH scoliosis which requires some form of treatment, can experience an
initial set of emotions or feelings. If you require treatment for your scoliosis, and as you come to terms with
what is happening, you can expect to experience a range
of mixed emotions: the news can cause feelings ranging
from worry and fear to despair and sadness. Then again,
you may find you feel nothing at all, or that you feel confused or angry and ask 'Why me?'

It can be common to experience physical symptoms due to the stress of finding out that you have scoliosis, such as stomach upsets, headaches or fatigue. While you may find you think more about your health in general or constantly think about scoliosis—perhaps even denying or disagreeing that you require treatment—it is important to remember that there is no right or wrong way to feel. Everyone can react differently to the knowledge that they have scoliosis, and the different ways that one can feel is perfectly normal in the early stages.

REACHING ACCEPTANCE

It may be helpful to remind yourself that it is quite normal to experience any of the feelings you are experiencing, such as fear, anger, sadness, and anxiety, when you first find out you have scoliosis. Keep in mind also, that all these responses fade with time, as you reach acceptance—that is, you become ready to face up to your scoliosis with hope, courage and determination.

This may take some time, and you and your family may find that you need to get help from a counsellor to help you move towards accepting your scoliosis. You should not expect to come to terms with having scoliosis overnight; that would be almost miraculous. But try not to bottle up your feelings; talking can help you feel better as well as helping you reach acceptance of your scoliosis.

It is understandable to keep asking 'Why me?' As much as we may not like change in our lives, trials and challenges can take place at any time, and there is a lot we cannot control. The important thing is how you deal with your scoliosis treatment or, how you learn to cope with it, and to what extent you are able to bounce back from this experience. This is also termed as your resilience. So try to stay calm and focus on the reasons that you require treatment.

A lot of good will come out of a situation that you may initially feel is all bad; and you need to hold on to hope. As you undergo this experience, and as you find your way out of it, you may uncover aspects of yourself that you never knew existed: finding unexpected strength of mind; courage and compassion for yourself and even for others.

You need to stay focussed on the treatment you require, remind yourself of your strengths, and believe in your ability to take one step at a time with the guidance from spinal specialists and your parents, even if it feels difficult. Talk to other adolescents on a scoliosis forum who can understand what you are going through—this will also give you hope and help you realise that what you are experiencing is normal.

In the meantime, staying calm and trying to think constructively can help you cope with your initial feelings; remember particularly that scoliosis is a condition, not an illness. Most people with treated scoliosis go on to live normal lives, and their scoliosis has only minimal impact on them. Although it can be difficult to take the news of your scoliosis, particularly if you require surgery, the sooner you take the steps to have your scoliosis treated the better it is for you.

BODY IMAGE

Body image is your perceptions and views about your body, which can influence how you feel about yourself. Sometimes, with adolescent scoliosis, there is an obvious curvature of the spine, while in other cases, the scoliosis may not produce an obvious curvature. If you have an obvious curve, you may think a lot about how you look, or even compare yourself with others. At times, you may compare yourself unfavourably with others, which can lead to what psychologists call 'body image issues'— when you judge yourself based only on your looks. It is important to get help for this from a counsellor, who can help you view things differently.

If your scoliosis does not have an obvious curve, but you leave it untreated when it requires treatment, over time it can lead to a change in the appearance of your spine, which can sometimes lead you to experience body image issues. Each case is different and, whether scoliosis is obvious or non-obvious, your spinal specialist will advise whether you need treatment. The treatment recommended is designed to treat your scoliosis from deteriorating further.

Bracing for Adolescent Scoliosis

If you require treatment for your scoliosis, your treatment may require you to wear a brace to school. Most people can manage this fairly well and have no issues with it, and you may find you will do so as well. But some adolescents find wearing a brace to school can cause them to feel self-conscious, at least at first. This is because they feel peers may be judging them in some way, and indeed, sometimes insensitive peers *can* make you feel different. But your peers can also be supportive, especially if they know *why* you need to wear a brace to school.

In my case, I found that most of my peers were curious about why I had a brace on and so they stared at me. I coped by choosing to ignore their behaviour, and adopting a defiant approach: *'I will not let them bother me'; 'They have the problem not me'* and *'I am more than my brace'.* My teacher also explained about my surgery and why I had to wear a brace, which was helpful. I developed resilience, in that I did not allow my peers to worry me too much.

It's a good idea to stay around peers who are supportive of you and also to refuse to get upset. Remember to think positively about yourself and who you are as a whole person—scoliosis and bracing are only one part of you. You need to be kind to yourself and feel OK about yourself. Think of your entire self—you are more than just a brace and scoliosis. Remember that how you *look* does not determine *who you are* as a person. As I mentioned in Chapter 1, beauty comes from within a person and not how they look.

Also, remind yourself that you will not be wearing the brace for long; it is only temporary and if you persevere with wearing it for as many hours as is suggested by your specialist, it will be more successful than if you do not. It's almost like having to wear orthodontic braces to school for a limited time. Thinking in these ways will help you to eventually start rising above your situation— a good place to be. If you do feel troubled by your peers, however, you may want to ask your teacher to explain to the class why you are wearing a brace. If you don't want to do this initially, of course, that is OK too.

Remember that all your different feelings at this time are normal. But if things start to affect you a lot—for instance, you find you are unable to do things you could do before, or you cannot enjoy things you previously liked or you feel sad most of the time—you need to get help. I suggest you do not just ignore your feelings. Please consider talking to a school counsellor, your parents and supportive friends, or join a scoliosis forum. As you share thoughts and feelings with other adolescents going through the same experience, you will see that your responses are very normal.

SURGERY FOR ADOLESCENT SCOLIOSIS

If you require surgical treatment for your scoliosis, this can be a stressful time for you and your family, at least in the lead-up to the surgery. You may find that you think a lot about what it will all mean. Do not hesitate to ask questions of your parents and even your surgeon, who can explain what you can expect before and after surgery. The more information you have, the more reassured you will feel, and it is best to ask again if you do not understand something. You may decide to write down some questions for the next consultation, such as:

- how much time you will need to take off from school
- what will happen in surgery
- when you can get up and walk
- how much pain you may have
- what pain control you will have
- when can you resume with your sports activities
- when you can return to school.

Asking such questions may help you feel more confident before your surgery, as you will know what outcome to expect. Try to look beyond your surgery—you can still live a normal life. Surgery will mean some restrictions, but generally this will not impact your life, if you decide for yourself you will not allow scoliosis to affect you negatively—after your recovery, you will be able to do most things as before.

Remember that everyone is different in how they will think and feel. You may find that you do not think too much about your surgery and just go with the flow of things. But if your feelings continue to distress you and you have trouble concentrating, sleeping or eating, or you are excessively worried about surgery, it is a good idea to talk to a counsellor or your parents, or even to other adolescents on a scoliosis forum. At times, you may not feel like talking to anyone, which is OK too. When you feel up to it, you may want to talk about it later. Sharing your feelings will help you to feel better.

As your surgery draws closer, you may find that you naturally start to feel calmer and stronger; you may not realise at the time that you have been mentally preparing for it. You need to stay connected with nurturing friends and family all this time.

Hope and focusing on your strengths

Having hope and trying to view things in a positive way when you are facing surgery can prove helpful. It is all too easy to become negative when you feel stressed, and many people do, but you need to keep things in perspective. Focusing on what is good around you, will keep you in a positive mindset. Take comfort from the fact that you will have family and friends around you; that there are nurses and doctors who will make sure it is as comfortable an experience for you as possible; and that you will be able to get back to school in no time at all.

Think about your strengths and all the times when you have handled other difficult things in the past. What strengths helped you cope then? You may find you were *tough*, had *willpower*, were *courageous, persisted* and *did not give up*. Well, those same strengths can help you this time too—so do not forget them. It is only natural to feel some nerves about your surgery, but you may even find that you just breeze through the whole experience!

Remember, scoliosis surgery today is very different to what I had to undergo in the 1970s—it no longer takes a year to recuperate! For AIS surgery, you will generally be in hospital for a week. You will be able to walk and get out of bed, unlike when I was in the cast and had to lie in bed for three months after my surgery—I wrote my story so you could see how it was then compared to now. There are far more advanced pain control methods today. But remember, while you will need to tolerate some pain and stress, the upside is that you are going to have a straighter spine, be able to stand taller, look and feel good and be less likely to experience medical problems in later life.

COPING EMOTIONALLY AFTER SURGERY

One to two days after your surgery, you will be allowed to stand up and walk. Thereafter, physiotherapists will take you for a walk each day. As your up-time improves, you will be allowed to return home. After surgery, it is common to have many types of different feelings for a while even after your return home. Some people feel sad, angry or distressed immediately after surgery, as they have to learn to do some things differently from before or are slower than usual as they heal after their surgery. All these types of feelings will get better over time, as you recover from the operation and return to your normal self.

If you find that you continue to feel stressed, you can talk with someone, or you can write feelings in a journal or engage in gentle physical exercise like walking, which may help you feel better. You can try to relax in other ways such as listening to music or practising simple breathing exercises; I often talk to my clients in counselling about breathing exercises such as deep breathing. You may wish to imagine breathing in *relaxation* and breathing out all *tension* you are holding onto— while staying grounded in the here and now or the present moment. This means reminding yourself of what you can see, hear, smell, taste and feel with all your five senses. There are many different breathing techniques to help you stay calm. Another technique is to take slow deep breaths in, and then slowly breathe out, while thinking of the word *relax* on your out-breath.

COPING PHYSICALLY AFTER SURGERY

After your surgery you should ensure that you get adequate rest and sleep and eat a healthy diet. As your surgery heals, you will be able to stay up for longer periods of time. You may have some restrictions such as not lifting heavy items or avoiding bending and twisting motions. Over time, you will need to learn to do things differently in order to care for your spine and not stress it unnecessarily. It will be important for you to observe your restrictions to allow your spine the best chance to recover.

It is also important to look after yourself in other ways post-surgery. Expect to have good and bad days after your surgery—it is normal and OK. Each day, try to do something small that you enjoy, whether that involves listening to your favourite music or engaging in a hobby. Stay connected with your friends, as socialising can help make you feel more cheerful. You can also make a list of small things you can do each day, which will put some routine and structure into your day. But be realistic and do not try to do everything at once. While recuperating in 2010, I tried to organise all my family photo albums in one day—it was not a good idea and I paid the price for it!

RETURN TO SCHOOL AFTER SURGERY

As your spine heals, you will be able to go back to school and also engage in your favourite activities once again. You may find you require having shorter days initially, until you can stay up for longer. Everyone will have a different set of feelings on return to school. You may find that you feel somewhat nervous on your return to school, or you may find you do not feel anything—both reactions are normal. You may feel worried about restrictions you have or how your peers may view you, or you may feel concerned that you will draw unwanted attention to yourself. In my own story, earlier in the book, I explained how I felt self-conscious, when Dad dropped me as close as possible to my classroom, so I would not have to carry my heavy backpack after my surgery. I tried not to focus on this too much, but at times I did dwell on it, but hesitated to tell Mum and Dad. In hindsight, I should have talked to them, or at least someone rather than dwelling on and worrying about it.

Contact sports are not recommended after surgery. If you played such a sport before surgery, you may feel self-conscious about it or think it is unfair, or you may not think about it at all. Over time, however, you will adjust to any restrictions you have. You can still do most things as before and lead a normal life—so focus on this. Try not to let things bother you too much—scoliosis is only one aspect of your life. You need to learn to be strong, but ask for help if things continue to bother you.

POST-SURGICAL CARE

Surgeons do their part leading up to and during surgery, and you need to do your part to care for your spine once it has been corrected. It is important to take up suitable exercises to help strengthen your spine, when your surgeon has cleared you to do so. This will ensure your prognosis remains excellent. In the beginning, I was allowed to walk in a hydrotherapy pool and on land, and much later I was allowed to swim when my spine had sufficiently healed.

CONTINUING PAIN AFTER SURGERY

In some cases, even after surgery you may still continue to experience pain; in this case, your surgeon can refer you for what is termed 'pain management'; this means that you will learn about how to better manage your pain, through consultation with a team of people such as doctors, psychologists and other health professionals.

EMBRACING SCOLIOSIS: A SPECIAL PART OF YOU

By now, you have to think about embracing your scoliosis as a special part of you— you need to befriend it. It will be a part of your life from here on; so try to care for your scoliosis as much as you can. Scoliosis will impact your personality in many positive ways. Numerous studies indicate that when young people go through difficult times early on in life, they can learn to become very strong and resilient people.

Resilience means having the ability to *bounce back* from difficult situations. Some of you may already be this way. For me personally, I found undergoing surgery at the age of 13 years and having to look after myself from early on in life, I became an even more resilient person, with lots of courage and determination. I also did not allow scoliosis to manage me, but learned to manage it.

I will also say that from the time of your diagnosis, it is not a good idea to ignore any feelings of sadness or nervousness, or any emotions that distress you or stay with you for a long time and stop you from doing things you normally do. If you are experiencing difficult feelings or not coping, share what you are going through with your parents, a school counsellor or your doctor, all of whom can help.

From here on, there is no reason why you cannot live as normal a life as you want. After surgery, you can stand tall! This experience will have built special strengths for you—try to find them.

TIPS TO HELP ADOLESCENTS COPE WITH SCOLIOSIS:

* Accept your scoliosis—it is going to be a part of you.
* Face scoliosis with courage and determination—stay above your scoliosis; do not let scoliosis manage you.
* Stay connected with your friends and family and keep communication open.
* Take necessary steps for the treatment you require (ignoring it will not help).

- Think of your strengths to help you cope—you will also develop new strengths from this experience.
- Think about the positives that will come out of this experience, particularly if you require surgery (this may be difficult in the beginning, but will get easier).
- Remember, such an experience early on in life will build your resilience and make you a stronger person.
- Be kind to yourself—do something you enjoy each day e.g. listen to music or watch a movie, play computer games.
- Look after your diet, exercise and sleep.
- Join a forum and communicate with other adolescents—talking to others who are undergoing the same helps you identify with them and in turn, make you feel better.
- Talk to a counsellor.
- Look beyond your scoliosis—remember there is life after your scoliosis treatment!
- Have hope
- Get professional help

~⁓

CHAPTER 4

SCOLIOSIS AND EMOTIONS IN ADULTHOOD

'I was always looking outside myself for
strength and confidence but it comes
from within. It is there all the time.'

—ANNA FREUD 1895–1982

TRANSITIONING TO ADULTHOOD

MOST PEOPLE WHO ARE TREATED for scoliosis early on in life go on to live normal lives, while observing their restrictions. This is how my life was after my surgery in 1974: I recovered, but needed to observe some restrictions, such as not being allowed to twist my spine in any way, bend over to pick up things or lift anything heavy.

As I reached adulthood, my life naturally progressed as I began my career, met my partner, married and

started a family. It can be a normal response for someone with treated scoliosis, particularly those who had spinal fusion as the method of treatment, to view the next
phase of life with some trepidation, particularly as they
reach significant milestones in life and as stresses on the
spine increase. For women who are treated with surgery,
this can be at the time of starting a family, which I discuss in the section on pregnancy.

PARTNERING IN LIFE

When I met my future husband, and it was time for me
to disclose my condition I was initially apprehensive. It
is normal to entertain thoughts of rejection or aban-
donment as you speculate about how your potential
partner may view you—this can be the case with any
medical condition. But the anticipation may be more
worrying than the reality of the situation, as a supportive and caring partner will soon alleviate your doubts
or fears and accept you for who you are as a person and
not for what you have or do not have. You need to give
yourself time to get to know a person and allow the
relationship to develop. Of course, a relationship may
not flourish for a range of other reasons – for instance,
a partner is not the right choice for you—and if this
happens, it is important not simply to attribute it to
your scoliosis.

Pregnancy and Starting a Family

In the case of women, it can be common to experience some nervousness at the time you decide to start a family, as you anticipate the effect of any pregnancies on your spine. You may feel concerned about the need to manage the demands a pregnancy places on your fused spine, particularly if your scoliosis was treated by surgery, but don't forget that, in contrast to what my peers were told in 1974, it *is* possible for a person with treated scoliosis to have children.

It can also be common for parents to be concerned about whether their daughters can lead a normal life-style, particularly in terms of managing any pregnancies and even afterwards, managing a new family. Many scoliosis forums online have a thread on pregnancy and starting a family. Conversing with other women who are in this phase of life can in fact, help you see that many others share your feelings and concerns, and that your response is normal.

For this reason, you will need to make both physical and psychological adjustments at this time—demanding consideration of what you can or cannot do, how you will do it, and what supports you will require. My own story, earlier in the book, gave you a glimpse of my concerns at the time I was starting my family in relation to managing a young family, holding down a career and engaging in my other usual activities. After multiple spinal surgeries, it was extremely important for me to care for my spine and not place undue stress on it; I also needed to learn to say 'no' without feeling guilty.

PROGRESSION OF SCOLIOSIS AND EMOTIONS

Research indicates that if treatment is required, the earlier the treatment the better the prognosis. However, even with early intervention, scoliosis can sometimes progress over time. It can, in some cases, progress during a pregnancy, while other medical problems can also impact prognosis. If you need multiple surgeries, you may find there is an emotional toll on you. With such unexpected developments, you may well experience mixed emotions, including anything from a sense of injustice to reflections on mortality or the transience of life issues if further surgeries are required. In some cases, body image issues can surface once more.

If you require further intervention later in life, you may find that you experience a grief response like the one you may have had when your scoliosis was first diagnosed: shock, despair or disillusionment. Your loved ones will undoubtedly feel the impact of this, and they will need once again to reach acceptance, as they strive to adjust.

Experiencing such emotions, while common, must not rule you—it is essential that you stay determined, find a way forward and proceed towards intervention despite any setbacks; persevering with hope and focusing on your inherent strengths. For instance, if you had intervention for scoliosis at a young age, you have most surely developed *strength of mind.*

THE IMPACT OF OTHER MEDICAL PROBLEMS
Sometimes, other medical conditions can interact with scoliosis and compound prognosis: for instance, osteopenia (a disease where bones weaken and can easily fracture), arthritis and degenerative spinal problems, to name just a few. Such medical problems are out of your control, but it is sensible to think about preventative measures that may help you avoid them. Remember to take into consideration that there will always be factors in your control, and factors out of your control and perhaps even, unrelated to scoliosis.

You may find it helpful to remember that you *can* control certain things, while accepting that there are other things you *cannot* control. For example, in my case, I had structural problems and other medical issues that were not in my control, which required me to undergo multiple surgeries in adulthood.

THE EMOTIONAL IMPACT ON LOVED ONES
When further intervention is required, your loved ones may get emotionally impacted, as they have to adapt to

unwanted and sudden change in their lives. Partners may experience a sense of injustice and find it difficult to cope with the uncertainties of the future. The ensuing stress, if not well managed, can strain relationships, as the whole family tries to become accustomed to what may lie ahead.

Although my family managed to cope when I had my corrective surgeries later in adulthood, it certainly had an emotional impact on all of us. For instance, my children were required to adjust around my surgeries and hospitalisations, which meant having to adjust to not having their mum around, and taking more responsibility around the house—one positive outcome of this was that they learned to fare for themselves.

Managing your different roles

By this stage, you are likely to have many roles, in your working life and in your family. Your role as a parent, spouse, in the extended family, and your role at work will require readjustment if you need further intervention for scoliosis in adulthood. Extended family members need to be supportive and reduce the demands and expectations placed on you. You should not place any guilt on yourself in relation to your inability to live up to the expectations of family or friends. This can significantly lessen stress, as you attempt not only to accommodate your own limitations, but the demands of your environment.

Psychologists say that, when the demands of the environment start to exceed what a person can reasonably offer, one can experiences stress or distress. Being realistic with yourself in terms of what you can and cannot do and communicating this to family is essential in order to cope. It is best to surround yourself with supportive people, in the same way as I have already described for adolescents undergoing treatment.

Now a note on relationships in general: it is essential to avoid unhealthy relationships around you; to be with safe people with whom you can create positive relationships that help nurture you. You will need to lay down boundaries or set limits on your own exposure to people whose behaviours lead you to feel stress, in order to protect your physical and emotional health—be it friends, family or work colleagues—and there's no need to feel guilty about laying such boundaries.

WHEN LOVED ONES COPE, YOU COPE

In adulthood, how well your loved ones—that is, your partner and immediate family cope will influence how well you cope. Many research studies have indicated that a supportive partner and family make a great contribution to a person's coping. A supportive atmosphere will enable you to survive and thrive despite adverse circumstances. In most cases, when you have a supportive family and social group, and you remain optimistic in the face of adversity, you will find you adapt to your situation well and are able to rise above it.

Caring for your spine

From the time of the diagnosis of your scoliosis, caring for your spine is a *must*, particularly if you had surgery. After corrective surgeries in adulthood, I had to schedule all my daily activities carefully, including leaving time aside to engage in rehabilitative activities. Regular exercise will not only help strengthen your spine but, as many studies indicate, exercise can enhance your mood. Not stressing your spine unnecessarily and working on regular fitness activities are factors within your direct control and so you need to take charge of this. Looking after your diet and getting adequate sleep are also important measures that will help speed your recovery. Do not feel guilty if you have to put yourself first—it is what you need to do.

Managing residual pain

There will always be instances when even after further intervention, you continue to experience pain. This is termed 'residual pain'. In this case, your surgeon may refer you for pain management which can help you learn how to manage your pain levels effectively, such that pain does not have a negative impact on you. Pain management is normally undertaken in consultation with doctors, psychologists and other healthcare profession-als as mentioned previously.

CULTIVATING AN ATTITUDE OF ACCEPTANCE

If you decide to return to work after further surgery and are required to change how you perform your job, you need to cultivate an attitude of acceptance once again. Such an attitude will help you make better adjustments to your work. Having compassion for yourself and your limitations; being gentle and kind, learning to care for yourself at work, and reducing the demands you previously placed on yourself are all important. I found that I could let go any obsessive or perfectionist tendencies at work without compromising my attention to my responsibilities, once I cultivated an attitude of acceptance.

MAINTAINING HEALTH AND PSYCHOLOGICAL WELLBEING

Maintaining your general health and psychological well-being is vital for management of scoliosis throughout your life. Therefore, gainful employment and engagement in meaningful activities, such as community services or similar, can provide meaning and purpose to life, helping you care for yourself psychologically. For example, I became engaged in researching and writing on scoliosis after my surgery in 2010. I published a paper on scoliosis for mental health professionals in 2012, and now I have written this book. These projects, while extremely challenging, were meaningful and rewarding activities for me.

Meaningful activities can help assuage feelings of hopeless and helplessness. It is a good idea to designate a day every week to doing something you really enjoy, so that you look forward to a regular interest. This will also prevent motivation lags, which you may experience at times, particularly when you start to feel negative about your situation.

I will also say that, as far as managing on a day-to-day basis is concerned, besides engagement in rewarding activities, it is also helpful to stay grounded and experience the present moment as you go about daily activities. Dwelling on the past and worrying excessively are unhelpful thinking patterns. Practice staying in the present moment—this is something you automatically learn to do over time, as you live with scoliosis, which is a part of you.

Here is an example of how you can stay in the present moment: every time you catch yourself engaging in the past or the future: bring yourself mindfully to the here and now—non-judgmentally accepting and experiencing the presence of the moment—accept what you have or do not have. Allow yourself to face pain, or dark moments without judgment. Just embrace it, connect with your inner wisdom, and let the moment be. Practice inner peace and allow yourself to step up to anything you are facing.

I like to use mindfulness-based techniques, such as breath awareness, to teach clients to stay in the present moment, to embrace feelings while staying calm. You can do this by just being with yourself, focusing on your breath in, and then the flow of your breath out, being in touch with each moment as it unfolds without any judgement. Remember that everything passes; this too will pass. Connect with your innermost values and stay grounded.

PARTNER SUPPORT

If you are in a relationship, even as you are dealing with your scoliosis, it is important to care for your partner too, so that you can maintain a healthy relationship. Further intervention can be stressful on your partner as well as on you, but it is all too easy to be self-absorbed and minimise a partner's needs. That can end up straining your already stressed relationship. Investing in your relationship and spending quality time together will help build a strong and fulfilling relationship.

ASKING FOR PROFESSIONAL ASSISTANCE

It is important to recognise when you would need or benefit from professional assistance. Indications that your situation is starting to get the better of you include: when your day-to-day activities start to feel difficult; you feel anxious and stressed most of the time; your relations with others are impaired; work stress starts to build up; and you feel your general functioning is being impacted. It is helpful to talk to your doctor about a referral to an appropriately qualified mental health professional. Counselling can help you understand connections between thoughts, feelings and behaviours that may be contributing to your experience of stress, tension, and anxiety.

Alternatively, you may want to join a scoliosis forum for support. Scoliosis forums allow you to share experiences with others. The forums can help you see your situation is in fact normal, and your emotional responses are warranted. As my published paper shows, there is much psychological research to indicate the importance of a good social support network in helping people deal with stressful life events.

TIPS TO HELP ADULTS COPE WITH SCOLIOSIS:

* Remember that you are on a journey with scoliosis. Prepare yourself for unexpected change and accept the reality of it—after all, change is a part of life.
* Remember to be kind and gentle with yourself.
* Embrace your emotions—try to reach acceptance.
* Take charge of any further interventions—denial will not help.
* Stay determined so you can manage your scoliosis—do not let it manage you.
* Find your inner resources and strengths.

* Find positives in your situation—things could be worse.

* Cultivate an attitude of acceptance—some things are in your control, while others are not.

* Engage in fitness activities to care for your spine—this needs to happen all the time as a maintenance regimen.

* Engage in meaningful activities, such as gainful employment, community service acts, rehabilitative activities—they will help you focus outwardly rather than inwardly.

* Nurture yourself—do something you enjoy each day, like listen to soothing music or go for walks.

* Look after your diet, exercise and sleep.

* Take on relaxing activities, such as yoga or meditation.

* Stay connected to life—enjoy simple pleasures, smell the flowers, see the beauty of nature, be mindfully present with your partner and children.

* Look for gems in adversity (this may not be immediately apparent).

* Talk to nurturing friends and family or join a forum.

* Get professional help when you need to.

~⁀

CHAPTER 5

FOR PARENTS OF CHILDREN WITH SCOLIOSIS

'Nothing in life is to be feared. It
is only to be understood.'

—MARIE CURIE 1867–1934

PARENTS' AND FAMILY'S EMOTIONAL RESPONSE TO DIAGNOSIS

A WORD OF CAUTION FIRST: as you read this section, re-member once again that, when you or a loved one is diagnosed with a medical condition and you begin to gather information about it, you may feel overwhelmed at first. In fact, by becoming more informed, you are empowering yourself, reducing your apprehension and developing your understanding of what to expect. With that in mind, read on.

Many research studies indicate that the diagnosis of any medical condition causes an emotional impact both on the person diagnosed and their loved ones, as everyone tries to understand its implications. It is important to note too, that each person is different, their family situation is different and their medical situation is different. Hence, when your child is first diagnosed with scoliosis, the way that you and your family respond to your situation may be different to that of another family.

As the parent of a child who has scoliosis, your response to the diagnosis will depend on whether your child needs treatment and the type of treatment they require. Other things that will influence how you and your family feel may include, for example: the cause of your child's scoliosis; the type of scoliosis they have; their age at diagnosis; your child's personality; how you as a family respond and of course, the outcome of your child's treatment.

When a diagnosis of scoliosis is first made, that requires intervention, particularly surgery, parents can find they experience feelings similar to a grief response: initial shock, despair, disillusionment, guilt, or sad feelings, with associated anxiety. Adolescent scoliosis is a type of scoliosis which can first emerge or even accelerate during an adolescent growth spurt or at puberty with no obvious physical signs from before.

In the case of adolescent scoliosis, when you first find out that your child's spine, normal since birth, has started to curve and twist, you can experience shock and disillusionment, as you come to terms with the diagnosis and treatment implications. My parents certainly experienced shock when I was diagnosed with AIS, as I had no outward signs of scoliosis, and nor did I have pain or other symptoms that would have led to an earlier diagnosis. While some people with scoliosis may have symptoms, others don't experience any. Many research studies indicate that a child's progression from 'normal' to 'not normal' health can cause parents enormous grief.

Be aware of the siblings of your diagnosed child, as they too are likely to experience a range of emotions, which may go unnoticed as you concentrate on the child with scoliosis. This is completely normal, given the significance of the diagnosis and the time it takes for everyone in the family to come to terms with the full implications of the situation. Such responses are usually characteristic of the 'adjustment phase' and mean that, over time, you will adjust to the reality of the diagnosis and the treatment required.

At the time of my diagnosis, my mum told me that my brother and sisters had to adjust to the fact that they would lose their oldest sister and buddy for a whole year. Mum said they had refused to go to school the day I left, and mostly stayed by her side. In the midst of all that is happening, it can sometimes be easy not to see the impact on siblings and offer the support they need.

UNDERSTANDING FEELINGS OF GRIEF

Historically, psychologists have used grief models of loss and bereavement to understand response of the human brain to major medical illnesses or diagnosed medical conditions and the ensuing emotional response. These models have helped individuals to recognise their feelings towards immense trial, pain, loss and illness by providing a context to understand and manage their emotions. Author and psychiatrist Dr Elisabeth Kübler-Ross has outlined the five stages of grief, which are not a complete list and which people may experience in various orders:

1. *Denial*—an inability to accept the situation, feelings of helplessness or even a rejection of reality.
2. *Anger*—asking 'Why me?' Trying to make sense of the chaos and experiencing a sense of unfairness.
3. *Bargaining*— petitioning to higher powers so you can be free of pain or engaging in wishful thinking.
4. *Depression*— experiencing sorrow, anxiety or insecurity.
5. *Acceptance*— embracing reality.

Grief theorists recognise that these feelings can commonly be experienced not just at times of loss and bereavement, but also when terminal illness or a chronic medical condition is diagnosed. Psychologists acknowledge that individuals can experience any or all of these stages at different times and in many different ways. Some people can experience these stages on and off, or episodically, while others may experience other associated emotions, perhaps in milder forms, rather than grief.

All of these emotions are a normal response to the situation. It is helpful to try and stay grounded in the present moment, allow your emotions to come and go, and accept this is understandably a difficult time. It may be beneficial to talk to supportive friends or family or even to a counsellor. Talking about your feelings with other parents on a forum or a primary support network can prove helpful, at least in the initial stages of the diagnosis of your child.

UNDERSTANDING EPISODIC GRIEF

When your child's scoliosis requires surgery, you may find you experience grief not just at the time your child is diagnosed, but also when they have the surgery, immediately afterwards, or even when they return home from hospital.

My parents experienced something similar to a grief response at several points: at the time of my initial diagnosis; when I left to have my surgery; when the surgery took place; and when Mum left me behind once more after visiting me in Australia. I will say, however, that after their initial grief, both my parents coped as best they could in the circumstances—something most parents *can* do when necessity dictates. That is: *reach acceptance and take necessary charge.*

It is important to understand that when you experience episodic grief, the emotions can become intense— rising like a wave, peaking to a crest, and just as a wave does, eventually subsiding. Remember that you need to survive this experience, so stay calm for your child, for the family and for yourself—keep things in perspective and carry on. As Professor Jon Kabat Zinn, director of the Stress Reduction Clinic and the Center for Mindfulness in Medicine at the University of Massachusetts says, 'You can't stop the waves but you can learn to surf'. Remember, that you need to stay calm and carry on.

UNDERSTANDING FEELINGS OF GUILT

When your child's scoliosis is suddenly brought to light, you may find yourself feeling guilty that you did not identify the problem yourself. My parents, like many others in their situation, certainly felt that way. It is understandable, and yet unreasonable, to expect yourself to have identified scoliosis in your child independently—it is something beyond your knowledge. Just take comfort in the fact that the scoliosis has been identified and that you now are in a position to address it and ensure that it presents no major obstacles for your child. It is important that you do not berate yourself but, instead, exercise self-compassion; share your feelings with someone else, such as another parent in the same situation. This will help normalise your response. The general awareness and knowledge of scoliosis is slowly increasing in the community, and everyone needs to take responsibility for earlier identification.

ACCEPTANCE AND STAYING HOPEFUL

What is the definition of *acceptance*? The dictionary definition of acceptance is 'the act or process of accepting or taking something given to you'. Remember, acceptance does not mean pretending everything is fine. Instead, it is accepting the reality of the situation as it is, and taking responsibility to move forward in hopeful ways. When I was required to undergo multiple surgeries, I found that acceptance was essential to enabling me to cope with my circumstances—in the same way, you must reach acceptance and then help your child reach it too.

You can help yourself to move forward by staying positive and managing any stress you experience in healthy ways, such as taking time out for yourself, engaging in something you enjoy each day, organising necessary visits to healthcare professionals and looking at appropriate rehabilitation programs for your child, particularly if they require surgery. By 'staying positive', I do not simply mean engaging in positive thinking, but rather, *acknowledging* that this is a challenging situation, *staying* grounded and *taking necessary charge*. The term I prefer to use is *constructive thinking*.

Of course, to cope with your feelings and reach acceptance, each of you will do what works best for you at the time. For instance, you may turn to a primary support network, such as a forum or a local group you belong to, or you may want time alone, or you may just want to engage in solo activities such as physical exercise, reading a book or going for a walk.

FOSTERING A NURTURING FAMILY ATMOSPHERE

Fostering a nurturing and supportive family atmosphere greatly improves the chance of your child coping. When your child witnesses you employing coping skills, such as positivity, hope, courage and determination, it will instil hope in them. The message you need to portray to your child is that 'we will all get through this together, even though it feels difficult' and 'although you feel distressed about it all, step by step everything will work out for you'. When parents model an ability to accept the situation, the child will see this and in turn learn to find their own acceptance.

TAKING CHARGE OF INTERVENTION

Gathering as much information as you can on scoliosis will empower you and better equip you to take charge of the situation. This may be in the form of discussions with your local doctor, browsing reputable sites on the internet for information on scoliosis, talking to your surgeon, or contacting organisations, professionals or medical specialists that your doctor recommends for support.

That said, it is not your sole responsibility to find out all about your child's condition. Your primary healthcare professional can provide you with ample information about the condition and about what needs to happen and when, so you do not have to worry about trying to find out every single piece of information on scoliosis. Understand that there is a point beyond which further information will not benefit you, so try not to get caught up in over-researching your child's condition. Instead, with the information you have, work towards achieving your end goal.

It is also a good idea to encourage your child to consider starting treatment earlier than later. If treatment is recommended and not undertaken, the risk is that the child's scoliosis may worsen over time, which may interfere with their daily life, and can require intervention such as surgery, that is often a more intrusive means to achieve the correction. Research indicates children with obvious scoliosis, or scoliosis that is progressing, may experience severe body image issues over time, which can impact negatively on their self-esteem. This is, of course, another good reason to consider earlier intervention.

UNDERSTANDING THE DEVELOPMENTAL STAGE OF ADOLESCENCE

Adolescent scoliosis, as the name implies, is normally detected around early adolescence—a developmental stage in life when many physical and psychological changes are occurring. Some issues adolescents are tackling during these years can relate to:

* identity and self-concept formation
* independence and autonomy
* identification and acceptance by peers
* experimentation behaviours(e.g. smoking, drug-taking)
* early dating
* concerns about physical appearance.

When some form of intervention is required for scoliosis, adolescent issues can be further compounded. For some adolescents, the whole experience can cause stress and anxiety, as they struggle to come to terms with their newly diagnosed scoliosis.

As far as surgery is concerned, some questions your child may have in mind can relate to:

* why they need surgery
* what surgery will mean
* what happens when they are anaesthetised
* how much pain they will have
* perceptions of being 'different' from peers.

It can be helpful to get into a habit or a pattern of communication about scoliosis, to help your child deal with their concerns from the time of diagnosis. Each family is unique in terms of personalities of members and interactional styles. So, while how each family communicates will be different, it is a good idea to try and keep communication channels open about any concerns your child and their siblings may be dealing with. Sensitivity and empathic listening skills are needed.

If you feel that your child requires professional help in managing their response to the diagnosis, encourage them to arrange to talk with a psychologist or social worker or even a school counsellor. Many research studies indicate young people have poor help-seeking behaviours for the reason that they do not want to feel different from their peers; you can read about this in my *Australian Journal of Counselling Psychology* paper. I will outline how you recognise symptoms which indicate they need professional help in Chapter 6.

ACKNOWLEDGING ADOLESCENT AUTONOMY AND INDEPENDENCE

Research indicates that young people experience a keen desire to separate from parents during the developmental stage of adolescence, and they often seek autonomy and independence as they attempt to establish their own identity. Hence, it is also good to acknowledge your child's opinions and wishes in relation to their treatment for scoliosis. In any decisions you eventually make for forthcoming interventions, they need to feel that you understand their feelings and that they were a part of the decision-making process.

For younger children, this is not normally an issue—you can usually take full charge of everything. Younger children, in general, have the tendency to just go with the flow of things and may be oblivious, either through naivety or natural resilience.

HELPING YOUR CHILD DEAL WITH BRACING

Encouraging your child to comply with the bracing treatment is important for this method to be successful. Research indicates that some adolescents choose not to comply with bracing, which may be due to discomfort;(in which case, seek out brace specialists to adjust the brace); or a feeling of shame over what they perceive as their schoolmates' perceptions about their brace.

While some of these studies indicate adolescents can feel self-conscious with bracing, other studies have indicated bracing has no impact on the child emotionally. But keep in mind, every child is different and will respond differently. How does your child feel about wearing their brace at school? Ask general questions to find out whether they are feeling awkward and, if so, remind them the brace is only temporary and that how they are viewed by others is irrelevant; it is how they view themselves that is important.

In my case, I was required to wear my polythene jacket to school for a period of time, and the teacher had to explain to the class about my surgery. It may be helpful to discuss with your child whether they feel it would be useful for the classroom teacher to create awareness and an understanding of scoliosis among the child's peers. In some, but not all cases, this can prove beneficial; discretion is advisable, as every child is different and will therefore perceive this differently.

NORMALISING YOUR CHILD'S EXPERIENCE

Many research studies support findings that identification with significant others who are undergoing same experiences can help normalise a person's experience. The girls and I at Margaret Reid hospital did not worry much about going from one plaster cast to another, which was remarkable, especially when you consider the fact that the cast was on for three months at a time. Surely ignorance is bliss! But, more importantly, our identification with each other helped normalise our feelings.

My experience is an excellent example of the value of identifying with peers who share similar circumstances; if your child is able to do so, it may allow them to accept what they are experiencing as 'normal'. Remind them that they are not the only one dealing with scoliosis;

encouraging them to chat on a forum, for instance, can prove beneficial.

Having the same experience as other inpatients at Margaret Reid Hospital, sharing feelings, having supportive nurturing friendships, and being able to identify with others—all helped to get into a more positive frame of mind, in turn enhancing my ability to cope.

Psychologist Martin Seligman, a guru of positive psychology, says that the cultivation of positive emotions helps an individual not only thrive but survive and flourish. At Margaret Reid, sharing our extraordinary experiences with the girls not only helped us share a special bond but led to cultivation of more harmonious relations.

HELPING YOUR CHILD BECOME RESILIENT

What is resilience? It is the ability to 'bounce back' from adversity—to stay grounded—and it is the most important thing you can help your child to build. Your child may be naturally disposed to be resilient, and in fact, studies indicate that most adolescents do naturally bounce back from adversity. So, it can be beneficial to remind your child of their mental toughness, their ability to take on challenges, to strive and to achieve goals in life, such as sporting or other activities that they may not think of immediately. You may also be able to draw on times when they managed to survive something difficult which can help them focus on inherent strengths, even while they are in the middle of a 'crisis' situation.

Your child may also find it helpful to think about someone important to them—someone they admire, or a famous person such as a celebrity or movie star—who faced adversity, and how they coped with their circumstances. Seligman's influential book, *The Optimistic Child* (which I recommend), discusses teaching children skills of optimism to help combat setbacks in life, while identifying existing positive strengths. It is also helpful to indicate to your child that this experience, in and of itself, can be a positive thing for their character, most importantly, building their resilience and cultivating a strong, confident personality. Your child may not, however, be able to think like that in the beginning—naturally not.

ADVANCES IN MEDICAL SCIENCE

I think this is the single most important message I wanted to convey to young adolescents and their parents when I decided to include my personal story—to indicate how far medical science has advanced since the 1970s and still continues to advance. I was allowed to stand up in intensive care two days after my surgery in 2010, and was ready to go home after ten days in hospital, quite unlike my surgery in 1974!

BUILDING YOUR OWN RESILIENCE AND INNER STRENGTHS

We can often forget our inner strengths when faced with adversity. You may need to search deep inside to find it. We all have gems—not only through having gone through difficult times but inherently; that part of you that is the observer self; it has unmovable strength and character. I found that reminding myself of my inner strengths helped me cope.

You can think of times when you experienced adversity or coped with a difficult experience. How did you do it? At first, you may have been anguished or apprehensive, or you may have felt like giving up, or you may have just decided that you had no other choice but to persevere and cope. My point is that, somehow, you must have *stayed grounded*. You need to find those same inner strengths yet again. Why is this important? Not only will it remind you of your inherent ability to cope but instil hope when you most need it.

In my practice, I often highlight inherent strengths a client has underestimated; such as belief in oneself, taking charge even when clouded by emotion, reliance on spiritual faith and staying power, to name only a few. Our in-built strengths can contribute to our resilience. When children witness a parent modelling resilience, it can contribute towards building resilience of their own.

If you do not think you have gone through any difficult times in the past and this is the first time you have been required to draw on inner strengths, it's OK: through this journey, you will develop them. In the meantime, you need to keep things in perspective, allow painful emotions to ebb and flow, take charge of what you can, connect with supportive family and friends, stay grounded and talk to a professional as necessary. Remember, through the negatives also come positives:

* you can grow to be an even stronger person
* your ability to step up to adversity will increase.

I mentioned the resilience of my children earlier in the book. I firmly believe my own responses to difficult life circumstances greatly contributed to their resilience. Remember that resilience can develop in many other ways, not only through direct experience of adversity. While I was naturally resilient from a young age, my Mum and Dad were also good role models for me, from *accepting life* and *adjusting my sails,* to *living fully in the present moment* —the essence of mindful living.

RELIANCE ON GOD

Many research studies indicate that reliance on God (whatever your faith) can also help cope with difficult times, contribute to resilience, and act as a buffer against stress, anxiety and depressed moods. My parents relied deeply on their Christian faith to help them cope with the trials they faced, and they encouraged me to do the same. I found a reliance on my Christian faith helped me greatly. But some people may find they initially feel angry with God, and even ask 'Why me?' Each person's response will be different, and what works for one person may not work for another. Once you have searched for meaning in the experiences you are going through, it is helpful to try and move forward.

As a Christian to other Christians, let me say the following: ultimately God is the greatest healer of us all. We need to have faith in God and trust him, in any and all circumstances. As Christians we know that trials are a part of our lives, and that through these trials God reveals his divine plans for us, which is not always immediately obvious.

Trials play an important part in a Christian's life, in anyone's life, really. It builds character, moulds us, teaches us perseverance, allows us to exercise hope, faith and trust in God. But we need also be mindful that as Christians, while we rely on God, we still have a responsibility to seek appropriate medical treatments through physicians and other professionals that God has placed in our lives. God can work through these professionals to heal and restore us when we place our trust in him. Many research studies indicate a reliance on God acts as a protective factor for people, which means that it can help people to cope with difficult times in life with *hope* as they keep faith in God.

HELPING YOUR CHILD COPE EMOTIONALLY WITH SURGERY

As far as surgery is concerned, you may find the most difficult time is coping emotionally as surgery draws closer. It is common to experience heightened emotions once again, coping not only with your child's anxiety but your own. You and your child can experience concerns in relation to returning to school, surgery itself and post-surgical restrictions. However, you will start to feel calmer when you have obtained all the information you need and can make decisions about proceeding towards your child's surgery.

In general, most of your emotions will settle after the surgery. Remember that your *perceptions* and *interpretations* of the approaching surgery may provoke more anxiety than the intervention itself. So, keep things in perspective, and be aware of how you are interpreting things. Try to think constructively, telling yourself:

* *I will take one step at a time.*
* *I am doing the best I can.*
* *I can get through this.*

In doing so, you are modelling coping skills to your child. Constructive thinking is different from positive thinking, which, understandably, can be difficult at this time. While you cannot physically support your child during the surgery itself, you need to show strength of mind and instil a sense of hope in your child—if you *give* your child hope, you can be sure they will *have* hope. Many research studies indicate that children absorb parental emotions and can even read the 'air' around you.

You have already seen how, as a child, I tried to comprehend *why* my Mum was in despair when she first found out I had scoliosis. As a matter of fact, I was continually 'reading' my parents and my siblings and taking cues from them. After her initial grief, Mum tried to be strong for me and gave me hope—in hindsight, one of the most important things she did was rely on her Christian faith which helped guide her through a difficult and challenging situation.

CONSIDERING THE PRACTICAL ASPECTS OF SURGERY

At a practical level, you will need to: organise finances for treatment; plan hospital visits; juggle family and work responsibilities; and arrange leave from work, such that you can care for your child on discharge, and until they are able to return to school. You may find that your role and responsibilities in the family alter, or your relationships become strained, at this time, as you accommodate the needs of your child after their surgery. Keep in mind that this can be a stressful time for siblings, who will require support, and for you, too. Requesting help—mutual share, care and support will go a long way at this time. Paying attention to your diet, getting good rest, and keeping yourself fit are all necessary.

HELPING YOUR CHILD AFTER SURGERY

After surgery, your child may experience a range of different moods. This can relate to the after-effects of surgery, the effects of pain medication, or sheer psychological and physical exhaustion. Painkillers may make the child drowsy much of the time, and sometimes, the side-effects of medications may distress the child more than the discomfort of surgery. The most common side-effects of pain medications can be bowel disturbances and nausea, the latter of which can cause appetite fluctuations. Discuss with the nursing staff how best to relieve such side-effects. Some children, on the other hand, do not notice any side-effects and will manage as well as can be expected. Try not to communicate your own anxieties, as children can easily pick up on them.

Now, a word on managing pain levels: I found it helpful to keep a pain diary at the time I had my surgeries in adulthood. You can keep a diary on your child's pain levels, and provide feedback to their doctor, so that the doctor can adjust pain medications as necessary.

EMBRACING PAINFUL EMOTIONS

In his book, *The Happiness Trap,* Dr. Russ Harris, a medical practitioner, therapist and executive coach, writes about accepting painful emotions and making room for them. He states that the core principles of acceptance can be captured in the Serenity Challenge, which is his version of the well-recognised Serenity Prayer: 'Develop the courage to solve those problems that can be solved, the serenity to accept those problems that can't be solved, and the wisdom to know the difference.' He goes further, saying that when you are faced with painful life circumstances, you need to not only make room for painful emotions, but also acknowledge your deeper values in life, as this will help you to stay grounded and connected to the present in meaningful and purposeful ways. As you attempt to reach acceptance, you need to be gentle with yourself. Russ goes on to promote the importance of action—acceptance and action go side by side, of course once your child has a diagnosis of scoliosis, you will need to take necessary action.

ACCEPTING AMBIGUITY

While we all like to have certainties in life, the truth is that there are a lot of uncertainties. We need to learn to embrace change and ambiguity, rather than stressing about what is a natural part of experience. It can be helpful to try and accept your uncertainties: notice your thoughts and feelings, do not struggle with them, but accept them for what they are and stay connected to the present. This is what Buddhist philosophy terms *mindfulness.*

If your child requires surgery, the fact that you experience some uncertainties as their surgery draws closer does not mean the results of intervention will *be* negative. Research indicates that, in general, prognosis for adolescent scoliosis surgery is excellent.

DEALING WITH EXCESSIVE WORRIES

Some ways to cope with excessive worries are to stay above your circumstances by exercising optimism, cultivating hope, managing worries by thinking through your problems to reach solutions, having good social supports and having an attitude of *'we will stay hopeful'*, *'we can cope with this'*, and *'you can do it'*. Regular engagement in activities that you enjoy, by yourself or with family members, can be helpful as you look forward to something pleasant each day. All these are important elements in achieving a sense of wellbeing.

Acknowledge that, after your child's diagnosis, many types of thought will arise. Psychologists often say that it is not the *event* as such that causes one to feel stress, but our *interpretation* of the event, that is the determining factor. Try to identify your thoughts—helpful or unhelpful— and observe those that are unhelpful. Let your thoughts come and go—do not engage with them or fight them.

Psychologists can frequently utilise imagery to help cope with unhelpful thoughts, based on an acceptance approach. Steven Hayes, Professor of Psychology, University of Nevada, gives consideration to the use of metaphors—so, you can observe unhelpful thoughts as dry leaves in a stream that just float past, or clouds in the sky that come to pass. Taking the perspective of an observer means that you let these thoughts come and go, and tolerate their presence without engaging with them. Hayes says that managing unhelpful thoughts can allow one to stay focused in the here and now, allowing one to take charge of the present—not getting caught up with useless thinking.

Russ Harris espouses giving distressing thoughts a label or description—such as '*here come the anxious thoughts again*' or '*the sad thoughts are arising*'—as a means of detaching oneself from the thoughts. At the same time, he advises remembering to stay grounded and experience the present moment, as you go about day-to-day activities. It is so easy to get preoccupied with thoughts and fail to smell the roses.

These are some examples of simple exercises that can help you cope with difficult thoughts, but a psychologist or another appropriately trained mental health professional can instruct you on specific stress management strategies to help you deal with excessive worries.

TIPS TO HELP PARENTS COPE WITH A CHILD WHO HAS SCOLIOSIS:

* Try to reach acceptance i.e. embrace your child's scoliosis and teach them to embrace it—it will be

a part of your lives. Remember it is not an illness. Your child can still lead a normal life.

* Learn to manage your emotions— keep things in perspective.

* Take charge of what is in your control.

* Read, learn, gather information— it will help empower you.

* Ask questions of the medical professionals and ask again for reassurance or clarity. You can be clouded by emotion and ask the same question repeatedly—that's OK.

* Take responsibility for intervention once you have enough information. Trust yourself. Make timely decisions.

* Have hope, find your inner resources.

* Listen to your children and foster nurturing interactions with each child.

* Work on psychological flexibility—be present with your difficult thoughts and emotions but take necessary action.

* Catch negative or unhelpful thinking—let it come and go; don't engage with it.

* Engage in meaningful activities, e.g. work or community services.

* Nurture yourself—engage in a pleasant activity each day, even if only for a short period.

* Look after your diet, exercise and sleep. Exercise helps release endorphins—psychologists term this 'happy hormones', which can lift your mood.

- Connect with nature—don't forget to smell the roses.
- Surround yourself with supportive, nurturing people.
- Share your experiences with a primary support network (e.g. a forum).
- Engage in counselling.

CHAPTER 6

RECOGNISING COUNSELLING NEEDS

'Knowing yourself is the beginning of all wisdom.'

—ARISTOTLE

EMOTIONAL HELP FOR ADOLESCENTS

THROUGHOUT THIS BOOK, I HAVE described times in your child's journey with scoliosis when counselling may become necessary. I have also written about the times when it may impact you and your loved ones and potentially lead to psychological and emotional problems. So, now you have some idea the situations or times when it may warrant professional help, and why you need to be aware of them. To recap, your child may need counselling at the time of the initial diagnosis, the time of intervention, such as bracing or surgery, and then after surgery as they make the necessary adjustments. At all these times, while your child's response can be a typical response to their situation, they can be encouraged to seek help.

UNDERSTANDING INDIVIDUAL DIFFERENCES

It is important to keep in mind that each person has a unique personality style, which simply means that each child's personality is different to another. In the same way, each person's medical situation is also different. All these factors when combined with your family's response style to diagnosis and treatment, will ultimately determine your child's personal experience of the treatment of their scoliosis.

RECOGNISING THE SYMPTOMS

How you actually recognise whether your child is coping or not coping is not just via how they think, feel and behave, but also via physical symptoms they report. Many studies indicate that, when younger children have difficulty coping, they often display physical than psychological symptoms, such as stomach upsets or headaches; you need to be alert to this. Having said this, in general, the younger the child, the more oblivious they can be to issues that might otherwise stress an older child.

While there is a range of symptoms that can indicate your child is not coping, these symptoms may also be a normal response to the diagnosis of AIS, bracing, surgery and hospitalisation, as indicated earlier. Therefore, it may not be as easy to identify whether your child's response to the diagnosis is a normal response, or if the symptoms indicate an inability to cope.

I have mentioned elsewhere in this book that your child's response to their situation or their initial feelings is likely to be a 'normal' response. When I write that your child's initial emotional response to the diagnosis is normal, however, this does not mean your child may not still need help. You may for instance, be alert to any unusual thinking styles, such as whether they are mostly negative about things or mostly anxious or worried and withdrawn since diagnosis. As children reach adolescence, they do not necessarily discuss thoughts and feelings readily, you may just need to be observant of this.

In general, be alert to any changes in their behaviour, thoughts or moods, such as:

* frequent sad feelings
* worrying thoughts or excessive preoccupation of thoughts
* irritability or anger
* withdrawals
* not partaking in activities previously enjoyed

* sleep and appetite changes
* feelings of hopelessness
* negativity
* refusal to go to school.

This is not an exhaustive list by any means, but as a general rule, any changes in your child's behaviour or moods that is affecting how they manage on a day-to-day basis, can be indicative of the need for further assistance, especially when symptoms continue in frequency and intensity over and above the initial adjustment period. This will of course, vary by personality, coping styles and so on.

There are many useful websites that provide consumer information and education on various mental health conditions and other psychological problems, including, how to recognise symptoms which indicate you need to consult a general practitioner or obtain help from a mental health professional. For instance, Australian websites you may wish to familiarise yourself with are: Beyondblue, Headspace, ReachOut and the Black Dog Institute.

ADOLESCENTS' LACK OF HELP-SEEKING BEHAVIOURS

Child and adolescent psychologist, Dr Michael Carr-Gregg, states that adolescents in general have poor help-seeking behaviours, and will not readily seek help in order not to feel different from peers. Significantly, while you may need to encourage your child to engage in counselling, you need at the same time to be aware that adolescents often desire not to be different to their peers, and so they may be reluctant to do so. Research studies also indicate this is a developmental stage in life when adolescents naturally desire autonomy and independence (as discussed in Chapter 5).

If you are unsure whether your child requires professional help, you can discuss it with your general practitioner or a mental health professional; or contact your local community health centre or another organisation for child and adolescent mental health. If your child is reluctant to attend counselling, you may consider attending counselling yourself, so that you can better understand how to help them.

USING SCOLIOSIS FORUMS

Conversing on a forum with other adolescents can provide a place to discuss feelings and experiences with others undergoing the same. This can help normalise emotional responses, while still providing a level of anonymity, particularly for those adolescents with poor help-seeking behaviours. Previously, I mentioned studies that indicate the natural resilience of adolescents. However, it needs to be kept in mind that with the physical and psychological changes occurring at this developmental stage of life, together with forthcoming interventions, it can predispose some children to significant emotional stress. Forums are a modern-day equivalent of how my peers and I coped at Margaret Reid Hospital all those years ago.

You also need to recognise times when your child naturally demonstrates good coping skills. Offer praise in these instances, as it will help reinforce and foster your child's coping behaviours. Psychologists often talk to parents about praise as a reinforcer for appropriate behaviour.

Emotional help for parents

Most people find they can make good adjustments initially, with the support of only their primary networks, such as friends, family or forums. If you feel that you are managing, you may not need to get any further assistance. Keep in mind that each person and their family's response to the treatment of scoliosis will be different, and may or may not be shared by other families.

If, after the initial adjustment period you find you continue to experience symptoms such as sad feelings or worry, hopelessness, loss of interest in activities enjoyed previously, disrupted sleep and appetite changes to name a few, that increases in severity or frequency and starts to impact day-to-day functioning, it can indicate need for professional help.

A trained mental health professional can assist you to develop strategies to cope and manage your situation better. They are able to assess your situation in depth, looking at contributory factors which are making it difficult to cope. Factors that can sometimes precipitate stress and compound ability to cope are: current stressors such as work and family stress, personality characteristics, trauma or past history, other unresolved issues, partner relational problems or any other mental health problems.

The health professional can teach you specific stress management strategies, for instance, understanding connections between thoughts, feelings and behaviours that lead to stress, anxiety and tension or instruct on structured problem solving to help cope with other specific stressors.

Remember that you do not need to wait until you are experiencing symptoms before you seek counselling; it can be helpful to share your feelings with a counsellor in any case, to help you manage. You may decide to start by talking to your general practitioner, who can make an appropriate referral. You can choose to seek support for yourself alone, with your partner, or for your family as a group (this is known as 'family therapy').

SELF-CARE

Engagement in behaviours such as physical and/or recreational activities, relaxation therapy such as yoga, meditation, or other specific stress management skills can help you care for yourself. Additionally, gainful employment or contributing to some form of community service activities can help you find meaning and value in your life enhancing wellbeing. I will add that, apart from my two boys, who give me daily inspiration to stay above my circumstances, resuming my career gave me meaning and purpose, allowing me to focus on something other than my scoliosis. If you allow it, scoliosis can spread through your life slowly and subtly and impact in many ways.

FOCUSSING ON YOUR CORE VALUES

Russ Harris indicates that, to cope with painful circumstances in life, we need to connect with our core values which can help us to stay grounded, while giving meaning and purpose to life, allowing one to mindfully connect to the here and now. Needless to say, this experience in and of itself made me an even more empathetic psychologist, who is passionate to inspire others to stay above their circumstances.

CONCLUSION

By now, I hope that you have developed a deeper understanding of the psychological and emotional implications of scoliosis for both the person diagnosed and their loved ones. Each person's journey with scoliosis is different, and since our life experiences are different too, we will all deal with scoliosis in our own personal way. Eventually, each of you will find your individual paths to help cope with your scoliosis and live well with it. Scoliosis will become a part of you—you need to embrace it.

Finally, it is my hope that Australian psychologists will conduct further research to advance the understanding of the scientific and psychological aspects of scoliosis and its impact on individuals, parents and loved ones. In years to come, I hope to see the Australian community better understand and become more aware of how scoliosis affects individuals and those close to them.

To the reader, I hope I have been able to touch your lives, even if just in a small way. I hope, too, that you are encouraged to face up to your scoliosis—or your child's— with hope, courage and determination. Remember to look beyond scoliosis— stay above your scoliosis, no matter what.

Be patient, for this experience will carve your personality in unique ways—you will become a very special person. As Helen Keller said, '*Character cannot be developed in ease and quiet. Only through experience of trial and suffering can the soul be strengthened, ambition inspired, and success achieved.*'

~

PART III

CHAPTER 7

OTHER PERSPECTIVES

'Keep your face to the sunshine and
you cannot see the shadows.'

—HELEN KELLER 1880–1968

THIS PART CONTAINS PERSPECTIVES FROM my husband Yogi and my good friend, Sally

Parents whose children are diagnosed with scoliosis can often worry about whether their child will go on to live a normal life. Here, Yogi my husband recounts briefly, how I managed my scoliosis, over the years of our marriage including his perceptions and experiences married to me. With these perspectives, I hope to further be able to encourage you to face up to the treatment of your scoliosis with hope, courage and determination.

Sally was an inpatient with me at MROH in 1974. Although she was treated for a condition called Spondylolisthesis (forward slippage of vertebra over another vertebra), our treatment and recuperation in body casts were the same. Sally shares memories of our time together at MROH while we both were recuperating from surgery. I have to add here, Sally's great sense of humour also kept me going at MROH, whilst I was away from home. Despite Sally's extensive spinal treatment, she too went on to live a normal life.

YOGI'S PERSPECTIVE

Reshmi graduated in the same year as me from university, and I met her shortly afterwards. We were in our mid-twenties, ready for the next stage of our respective lives. We courted for a year before I proposed and, as history would have it, she succumbed to my charms. It was a time of bliss and an important milestone, as we now reflect on it, for her parents, who would have harboured concerns about whether their daughter would lead a normal life. We were married eight months later.

Before we married, Reshmi did mention that she had undergone surgery for scoliosis as an adolescent in Australia and that she had recuperated for a period of one year. Apart from her very upright posture (of which, had I had the same, my own mother would have been proud, given the numerous reminders she gave me to sit straight), I knew very little about any limitations Reshmi had, or even about scoliosis for that matter.

After our wedding, we settled in Melbourne and were soon busy setting up our lives and starting our careers. After two years, we decided to move back to Sydney, where we lived normal, contented lives. When our first son was born, apart from some additional discomfort with her back during pregnancy, which we considered a normal part of pregnancy, we were largely oblivious of the possible impact of scoliosis on our lives. The obstetrician was not too concerned with the election of a normal delivery and impact on a treated spine.

Reshmi made the decision, quite possibly while she was in labour, that if there was a next child, the delivery would be by caesarean section, and indeed our second child was born by C-section two years later. Until both children started school, Reshmi worked part time, before we chose family over career and she ended up rearing the two children. She would often be seen carrying one of them on her hip, as she went about her business of daily life, packing and unpacking the baby pram, attending playgroups and mums' groups, shopping, preparing meals and, basically, managing the household and keeping the boys entertained.

Life continued and both our careers kept flourishing as Reshmi too returned to work, and her scoliosis did not have any significant impact on us. Reshmi was under the supervision of specialists during this time, who kept a watching brief on her spine. Reshmi's scoliosis did progress, resulting in further intervention. By now, she was an established psychologist and was passionate about her work.

Our life seemed to change overnight and we consciously faced scoliosis for the first time when she had a sudden onset of pain in 2006. I did not know Reshmi when she had the interventions as a child, and she had probably been too young at the time to fully comprehend what was happening. We made an appointment with our GP, followed by a visit to the specialist, and after a series of X-rays and MRIs, we were informed it was time to consult a leading orthopaedic surgeon, as Reshmi might require assessment for additional surgical intervention.

This started a series of visits to the surgeon, where we received information on the condition, prognosis and intervention required. Each consultation provided us with more detailed technical information, but when we returned home to ponder the situation, we found we had more questions than answers. Sometimes we understood the explanations clearly, but at other times the information left us more confused.

The surgeon, like all surgeons, was highly trained, skilled and competent. His role was to provide us with information that enabled us to understand the condition, its progress and the intervention Reshmi needed. We recognise that the surgeon's primary role is to attend to the medical issue and that they are very much in demand, given the queues in their waiting rooms. Hence, in the limited time they have during a consultation, they focus on their primary task of managing the medical intervention and do not have the luxury of time to hold the hand of each patient and their families as patients go through the emotional rollercoaster of the diagnosis, its treatment and the impact it will have on their life.

Over time, Reshmi went through three cycles of intervention, which included three visits to theatre. During this period, given Reshmi's profession as a psychologist and her inherent qualities, she started to recognise that not only did she have these feelings of uncertainty, anxiety and trepidation of the unknown, but that many of the people she would see in the waiting rooms of the surgeon, in the hospital wards and the X-ray centres were experiencing similar feelings. She observed the parents of the many young adolescents there who were undergoing diagnosis and treatment and who were the same age as she had been, and she recognised their anxiety and concern about the future of their children, knowing that her mum had felt that way about her, many years before.

Having come through surgery, married and had children of her own, Reshmi resolved to chronicle her journey as a family record, to ensure that future generations will have more awareness of the condition and the need to be screened, given the evidence that AIS has a genetic component. Over time, her conscience led her to broaden her book's audience, with the aim of communicating not only with her family about the condition but with other parents and adolescents who would benefit from her particular experience not only of scoliosis, but also of the psychological implications of being diagnosed, undergoing treatment and living with the condition.

Although Reshmi originally also intended this book for other psychologists, who would then be better equipped to manage the needs of the parents and children in dealing with the diagnosis, treatment, management and comprehension of scoliosis over time, she met this objective when she published her paper in 2012. The primary focus of this book, then, remains the parents and children who are coping with scoliosis and whose anguish is heard on the various forums and chat rooms, as they struggle to come to grips with the diagnosis and its implications on the life of their loved ones.

Reshmi's book reassures family and carers that what they are feeling about their child's scoliosis is normal; that there is much that can and will be achieved; and that their feelings can be understood and managed. This book provides hope to parents, helping them to understand that scoliosis is not an illness but a condition, and that—even in very extreme cases such as Reshmi's own—it is possible to lead a full and productive life with scoliosis.

In a way, scoliosis acts as a 'voice of reason', advising caution when, for example, bending your knees to pick something up or considering whether to lift a heavy object, and encouraging you to keep fit and generally not give in to the condition. The surgeons will do their part in treating the condition and everyone else needs to contribute in keeping the balance as the person with the condition adjusts to their new-found 'partner' in scoliosis.

Reshmi continues to be a spouse, mother, and daughter, and she manages her career as a private psychologist. She is a very special woman, resilient to a tee, made even more special by her experience. She continues to use this experience of her journey to assist others in all walks of life, contributing in her own way to alleviating the anxieties of people who are adjusting to a new diagnosis or facing any adversity in life.

Reshmi: with the compassion, energy and dedication you have shown in writing this book, as you have in everything you do, I wish you all the best and my love in achieving your noble aim of reaching out to those in need of your wisdom and support and in advancing research on scoliosis in Australia.

SALLY'S PERSPECTIVE

In October of 1974, I was a tall, skinny, pony-club kid with a very sway back, bent legs, chronic pain and a chronic attitude of trust and optimism. On my horse, I had no pain and no restrictions—I could ride like the wind. We drove south from the warm sunshine and headed to Sydney for what we thought was a bit of surgery that would help me stand straight and take away the pain I had been living with for the past three years, as my spine slipped due to a spondylolisthesis—a broad definition of which is the forward slippage of one vertebra over another.

My family also did not really know how long we would be away from home. We lived on the Gold Coast, Queensland, and Dr Daymond was based in Sydney. So my Dad took eight weeks off work and organised a house sitter for our house and found a house in Sydney that we could occupy (house sitting) for the duration of my treatment. We had no idea that my stay would take four months.

My particular type of deformity was very uncommon and, as such, there was no preferred remedy other than traction every school holidays and a body cast and crutches in between. My father was not satisfied with this antiquated treatment and asked for a second opinion. The doctor took my X-rays to an orthopaedic conference, where Dr Daymond presented his new technique involving halo femoral traction, rods, bone grafts and immobilisation in a plaster cast for three months.

On the day of my admission to Prince of Wales Hospital, my mother and I were taken to the children's ward so that I could be shown the halo femoral traction that I would be attached to me the next day. I will never forget the horror of seeing a teenage boy lying there with bolts attached into his skull and through his legs, and re-alising that they were going to do that to *me* tomorrow. I tried not to cry, but it didn't work. Mum too was horrified, but told me that I just had to be brave, and that she would be with me all the way, and that it was only for two weeks. So, our hearts dragging on the floor, we returned to the adults' wing, where (at 16) I was the youngest patient.

The first half of the treatment was to be the same as Reshmi's, who was about four weeks ahead of me and already at MROH when I was admitted to the Prince of Wales.

These are some of my recollections from MROH:

ROTA-BED MEMORIES

Being on our tummies was better on the rota-bed, as it put us in a position (for four hours) where we could read, eat, play music on our cassette player, and generally be less useless, and more independent, than when we were on our backs staring at the ceiling or trying to position our overhead mirrors so that we could see our room-mates and surrounds. Being immobilised with the exception of our arms was a truly frightening experience. We were so flat that when we tried to feed ourselves we ended up covered in food—especially peas!

UNCLE LES

I met Uncle Les at MROH where we had to bide our time for the next three months (in my case), and I remember the gifts he brought us at Christmas. He had done the rounds of the pharmacies in the area and put together lovely padded wash bags full of lipstick, lotions, fragrance and nail polishes. What a treasure he was! I was particularly taken with the emerald green nail polish and asked the nurse to paint my toenails. We girls had a competition to see who could grow the longest toenails. This would be the only opportunity in our lives to do so, as we were immobilised. I can't remember who won, but I do remember my glorious green toenails!

THE GIRLS

I was happy to be with other girls who were going through the same experience as me. Reshmi and I became besties, and we laughed and cried together. My mum took up a position at the hospital and moved into the nurses' quarters, as Dad had to return home to keep his job. Mum took much delight in being Mum to my 'spinal sisters' who had no family nearby. She would buy us treats at the shop, do our washing for us, rub lotion into our sore bits and sit and talk.

BRAVE ATTITUDE

I was feeling sad and asking 'Why me?', and soon after my arrival I met a bright little button of a girl called Tina, who was only about four years old and could not walk. Another tot had brittle-bone syndrome and would never be able to live a normal life. It was then that I said to my-self, 'How lucky am I? I've just got a bad back and it won't be forever'. That day changed my life. To this day I often say, 'I'd rather have a bad back than a bad attitude, as a bad attitude is so much more debilitating'.

BODY CASTS

This cast was applied after I had surgery to have the halo femoral traction removed and the stainless steel rods in-serted. I was a skinny 54 kilograms when I entered hospi-tal, and the rigours of the first four weeks in traction and on the rota-bed caused me to lose another four. It was on this bony frame that my body cast was applied, and it didn't take long on the fatty food at Margret Reid for my weight to start increasing and my circulation to be cut off by the tight plaster, which started below my bust and continued down my right leg (the length of the plaster stopped it from moving up and down). The cast was cut down both sides with the rotary saw (very scary) and then reapplied with fibreglass casing to allow a wee bit of expansion. The fibreglass was scratchy and often caused a rash on my in-ner arms. As we all had to lie flat on our backs, it was not easy to slide in the special wedge-shaped bedpan.

HAIR-WASH DAY

We would beg the nurses to try to wash a little under our casts on hair-washing days, but they always said no. I kept counting down the weeks, days and hours until it would be time to have the plaster cast removed, which would allow me to get vertical and sit for the first time in four months.

THE FIRST STEPS

I remember being so excited for Reshmi when the day came for her to stand up, yet amazed that she had so much trouble in learning to walk again. I was convinced that when my turn came, I would concentrate so hard that I would be able to walk well, and that would enable me to go home to the Gold Coast to see all my friends, family and beloved horses again. How disappointed I was when my turn did come and my body reacted with swelling legs and shooting pains. I was determined to be strong and mobile, however, so I would raise my tilt-a-bed at night and walk from bed to bed, practicing so that I could go home. Boy, did I get yelled at when I got sprung by the sister!

I will never forget the day my plaster came off. It is still one of my most luxurious memories, the pleasure of being able to touch my own belly again after having it locked away for three months—a truly heavenly experience. Remarkable too, to see how much old skin came off when I was gently cleaned with a face washer—creepy but fascinating.

CHRISTMAS DAY

We had a happy Christmas Day, and I recall rolling around clutching my bulging tummy, which ached from all the food that had been put in, within the confines of the body cast. Groan! The next day we turned the news on and saw that Darwin had been blown away by Cyclone Tracy—this Christmas was one that Australia will never forget.

RETURN HOME

When I was able to walk the length of the ward, I was allowed to go home to continue my recuperation there. I was transported to the airport, where an air ambulance flew me back to Queensland. I was overjoyed to be back on familiar ground and still remember the delight at seeing my neighbourhood through the window of the ambulance as it brought me home.

BRACING

I wore my back brace for the next 18 months. When I went on dates, I became quite adept at wearing the brace out the door, before promptly taking it off and dropping it in at our neighbour's door, where I would pick it up again on the way home so I would be wearing it when my mum gave me her welcome-home hug. Sneaky, eh?

REMOVAL OF RODS

When I was 19, my first boyfriend came to Sydney and the Prince of Wales Hospital to support me in having my rods removed. The doctor said that the rods had done their job in supporting the bone graft, and that they could come out. I think I was only in hospital for a day or two, but I do remember being most insistent to Dr Daymond that he didn't give me another scar, to which he replied that I wouldn't see any difference, and he was true to his word.

MY LIFE SINCE SPINAL FUSION: 40 YEARS OF FITNESS, FRIENDSHIPS AND FUN!

With my spine straighter and stronger than before, I felt I was now well equipped to take on anything that life presented in the years to come. I was thrilled to get the first full-time job I applied for as a Veterinary Assistant, and full points go to my employers, who gave me a go despite the fact I was wearing a back brace. They didn't mind— what they wanted was my attitude and my enthusiasm more than a perfect spine, and so I gave them 110% and they gave me a hand with the heavy lifting (of large dogs) that was part of the job.

During this time, I had also found the Gold Coast Underwater Club, which taught scuba diving for only $30. My Mum and I rolled up for the prerequisite dive medical, which she passed and I failed—not because of my back, but due to the childhood asthma I had not quite shaken off. So Mum got to dive before I did, although I caught up the following year after swimming countless miles to build up my lung capacity. My back also grew stronger and, when I did get my diving certification, I had no trouble carrying the scuba tanks, which weighed 16 kilograms.

This new competency turned out to be the great passion of my life and led me and my reinforced spine to some extraordinary adventures, such as leading over-50 international adventure travel expeditions scuba diving off the islands of the South Pacific, Melanesia, Polynesia and Asia, wreck diving on Second World War shipwrecks, exploring the underground sinkholes of Mount Gambier, South Australia, snorkelling with whale sharks, diving with humpback whales, sea snakes, dolphins and sharks, and even exploring beneath the ice of a frozen lake in Cape Cod, USA.

My sturdy back enabled me to dive into the sea to help rescue a lady whose husband had been taken by a great white shark, which earned me a Bravery Medal. I now have the honour of being the National Vice President of the Australian Bravery Association, the aim of which is 'supporting those who risk their life, to save another's life, property or the environment'—a rare privilege I would not hold had I not had life-changing spinal fusion.

I did the research and found out that, if I was careful, I could also bungee jump, enjoy white-water rafting, explore underground caves, go mustering on horseback, enjoy the thrill of abseiling, go hard on the ski slopes and even skydive! A recent international dive expedition took me to a place where (although I had been vaccinated) I contracted typhoid fever, which attacked two of my vertebrae. So, I have had to curtail my thrill-seeking for the past year—but I know that my back, being the wonderful creation that it is, will once again heal and, given rest, time and plenty of hydrotherapy, I'll soon enough be gearing up for the next adventure that comes my way. The only thing that my back has ever prevented me from doing is hang gliding—I don't think my back would like those inconvenient unscheduled landings.

I am delighted to be able to assist Reshmi in her quest to bring understanding, acceptance, courage and confidence to those who read her story, and to encourage every person with a wonky spine to keep their chin up and know that it just may be one of the most valuable experiences of their whole life. I live by this mantra: 'I'd rather have a bad back than a bad attitude, as a bad attitude is so much more debilitating.'

If you have been told that you need a spinal fusion, proceed with confidence, knowing that you have access to the most fantastic resources, skills, innovation and modern techniques to set you up for an excellent recovery, the likes of which were beyond the wildest dreams of the handful of teenage girls I got to know in hospital in

1974. I wonder if I will have as much fun in the next 40 years as I have had in the first—I'll let you know.

Another funny thing I forgot to add is that I have always received compliments on my lovely posture—for standing so straight. It's true—there's always an upside!

REFERENCES

Dalai Lama, His Holiness the 14th & Cutler, H.C. (1998). *The Art of Happiness: A Handbook for Living.* Australia & N.Z.: Hodder Headline Australia Pty Limited.

Harris, R. (2007). *The Happiness Trap: Based on ACT—A Revolutionary Mindfulness- Based Programme for Overcoming Stress, Anxiety and Depression.* Australia: Exisle Publishing Ltd.

Harris, R. (2012). *The Reality Slap: Finding Peace and Fulfilment when Life Hurts.* Oakland, CA: New Harbinger Publications, Inc.

Kabat-Zinn, J. (1994). *Wherever You Go, There You Are: Mindfulness Meditation in Everyday Life.* New York: Hyperion.

Kubler-Ross, E. & Kessler, D. (2005). *On Grief and Grieving: Finding the Meaning of Grief through the Five Stages of Loss.* London and Sydney: Simon & Schuster,

Pal, R. (2012). *Psychological implications of scoliosis: Perspectives from adolescence to adulthood. Australian Journal of Counselling Psychology*, no. 1 (Autumn): 19–26.

Scoliosis Australia (2014), www.scoliosis-australia.org.

Seligman, M.E.P. (2011). *The Optimistic Child: A Proven Program to Safeguard Children against Depression and Build Lifelong Resilience.* North Sydney, NSW: William Heinemann.

Seligman, M.E. P. & Csikszentmihalyi, M. (2000). *Positive psychology: An introduction, American Psychologist,* 55(1): 5–14.

About the Author

Reshmi Pal is a registered psychologist in private practice in Sydney, Australia. She has more than 25 years of clinical expertise in adolescent, adult, family and couple therapy in both the public and private sectors. Reshmi graduated with Master of Education (Psychology) from the University of New South Wales in 1984. She is a member of the Australian Psychological Society, the APS College of Educational Developmental Psychologists and the APS College of Counselling Psychologists.

Currently, Reshmi works in independent private practice providing consultancies to a range of private sector organisations, individuals and other health and mental healthcare providers. She has a particular interest in supporting individuals with a new medical diagnosis and those with chronic health problems.

Reshmi lives in Sydney with her husband and two boys.

CPSIA information can be obtained
at www.ICGtesting.com
Printed in the USA
LVOW13s1745090317

526681LV00010BA/567/P